The Secrets of SUCCESSFUL BUSINESS MEETINGS

Gordon Bell

HEINEMANN PROFESSIONAL PUBLISHING

Heinemann Professional Publishing Ltd
Halley Court, Jordan Hill, Oxford OX2 8EJ

OXFORD   LONDON   MELBOURNE   AUCKLAND   SINGAPORE
IBADAN   NAIROBI   GABORONE   KINGSTON

First published 1990

British Library Cataloguing in Publication Data

Bell, Gordon, *1910* –
   The secrets of successful business meetings.
   1. Meetings. Organization
   I. Title
   658.456

ISBN 0 434 90247 0

Phototypeset by Deltatype Ltd, Ellesmere Port, Cheshire
Printed and bound in Great Britain by
Billings Ltd, Worcester

Contents

Preface

If you wish to rule the world like an Alexander, a Hitler or a Caesar, close this book at once and make your way to the nearest haven for the deranged. We aim to interest more sensible people who merely aspire to become the Chairman of ICI, or to manage a factory, a department store, even a department, or perhaps their own business – and to manage with more success than the next man or woman.

As their waists grow large and their hair grows thin, thousands of stuck-in-a-rut managers wonder what went wrong with their careers. Let them look to their meetings. Most of us have witnessed or have been involved in something like the scene that follows.

A group of managers quietly chatting about their problems in general were startled when one of their number brought his fist down violently among the coffee cups and, as one possessed, shouted: 'Meetings! Meetings! Perishing, flaming meetings!'

Peter: 'You frightened the life out of me, Harry. What about meetings?'

Harry: 'In my job, life seems to be an endless series of eternal meetings and most of them an utter waste of time. I need help.'

Peter: 'Don't we all?'

Diana: 'Well, you can always help yourself. There are plenty of books about meetings.'

Harry: 'Don't I know it. I've read three books about meetings in the last month.'

Roger: 'Well, now you know, don't you?'

Harry: 'Do I hell? Do any of you understand what is meant by amendment to a negative motion; or an

	unincorporated association; or kangaroo closure; or compositing; or integrated mandating?'
Roger:	'No. But would it make a ha'p'orth of difference to my business if I did?'
Harry:	'Of course not. Why can't somebody write a book about workaday meetings – board meetings, management meetings, project and production meetings, meetings with customers and staff – the sort of meetings we go to every day without stuffing us with jargon and procedures?'
Peter:	'Don't be silly, Harry. Got to have procedures and traditions in some places. Look at the House of Commons: six hundred odd collective egos all bobbing up and down and abusing one another. Got to have rules, otherwise they'd be slitting each other's throats, and instead of counting votes they'd be measuring results in buckets of blood. Be sensible, old man. Got to have rules.'
Diana:	'Of course we have. Imagine the Law Courts without rules and regulations.'
Harry:	'Perhaps you'd like the canteen committee to wear wigs and call each other M'Lud?'
Peter:	'When I was a member of the Students' Union Debating Society, we had very strict rules. I never really understood them, but there they were. The For the Motion people had their say; then the Antis cut them to ribbons, and so on. Attack and counter-attack. Battles galore. Great fun.'
Harry:	'Maybe, but that's not how I see business meetings – as two armies facing each other in entrenched positions, flourishing their prejudices and using every dirty trick to slaughter the enemy. Who wants his business to be a battleground where disaster for one side – even corporate disaster – means jubilation on the other side?'
Anne:	'Nobody does, I suppose.'
Harry:	'We don't want conflict; we want cooperation. We don't want warfare with people hating each other's guts. Even when we disagree, we all ought to be on the same side working for the good of the firm.
Peter:	'That pie in the sky, Harry. Even a Sunday school has

to have some discipline. So must business meetings. Otherwise they'd be just a shambles.'

Diana: 'Imagine what would happen at our annual general meeting with over two thousand shareholders behaving like a mob. Awful thought.'

Roger: 'The rules for an AGM are strict.'

Ann: 'They must work too.'

Peter: 'How about a political party conference? Or the annual trades union jamboree? They'd be chaotic without the right procedures and formalities.'

Harry: 'How about a parent/teacher meeting? How about a works safety committee? How about our managers' meetings?'

Roger: 'Oh, don't be an idiot. They're different. There are never more than about a dozen people at any of them.'

Harry: 'Exactly. The greater the number of people the more need there is for formalities and strict rules. I've never known an AGM to be chaotic. The Company Secretary supervises the arrangements. He's a specialist. To belong to the Society of Chartered Secretaries means that you've been rigorously trained to understand the legal requirements of the Companies Acts and the rules necessary to keep the firm out of trouble. Everything has to be strictly legal and formal. But that doesn't apply to most of our day-to-day meetings. What can we do to make our meetings less of a burden and more businesslike?'

This book is dedicated to the Harrys, the Dianas, the Peters, and Annes, the Rogers and all those who wish not only to succeed, but also to enjoy themselves in their workaday world of meetings.

1   Formalities

At the State Opening of Parliament, Her Majesty the Queen does not travel from Buckingham Palace to the House of Lords riding a bicycle. The Lord Mayor of London would be most upset if guests sat down to a Guildhall banquet wearing pyjamas. Neither would full evening dress, white tie and decorations be considered acceptable garb for a nudist colony. There is a time and a place for formalities. What a dull world this would be without splendour and tradition and an occasional reminder that we have much to be proud of. But grand processions do not pay the rent or get the washing-up done. A duchess leaves her tiara in the safe when she goes shopping: and we can leave most of the formalities attached to meetings where they belong – at formal meetings.

Parliamentarians need to be acquainted with such standard works as Sir Erskine May's *Parliamentary Practices*. They must know *The Manual of Parliamentary Procedures* (Sir Courtenay Ilbert). They must learn when to bend over to the Whips. 'Take away that bauble' ordered Oliver Cromwell, pointing to the Mace. The Mace has outlived Cromwell despite some modern efforts to knock it about a bit.

The antics in the House are frequently reminiscent of The Crazy Gang but, as long as the Speaker keeps his wig on, 'Order! Order!' prevails. Members of Parliament are not half so silly as they sometimes allow themselves to appear. They are splendid chaps who do most of the real work on committees – smaller meetings with fewer formalities.

In conducting its legally prescribed meetings, a large public company might get into serious trouble without the guidance of a qualified Company Secretary. He needs to know not only Common Law relating to meetings but also to master every old and new Act of Parliament relevant to his job. This is also true of leading trades union officials. They must be not only fully cognisant of the Trades Unions Acts and internal rule books, but be able also to disseminate that knowledge down to the grass roots.

There must be rules and constraints even for the most banal of television quiz shows.

Where there is a need to be formal, let us be formal: where there is not, let us devise common-sense disciplines that suit our daily business meetings, and work within them.

2 Why bother about meetings?

All learning exposes a wider field of ignorance. An apprentice seafarer might know by heart and fully understand every word in *The Manual of Seamanship*, but each day at sea obliges him to cope with imperative matters outside its pages. Lawyers, physicists, engineers, economists – qualified specialists in all disciplines – soon discover that the scroll handed to them on graduation day represents only page one, volume one, a few square inches in the vast acreage of knowledge needed in their professions. A medical man starts to learn when he faces his first patient. What goes before is necessary, but a basis – no more. We live and learn but we also need to learn as we live or become stagnant.

Let us not, however, undervalue solid foundations. Sir Winston Churchill recorded that he had an advantage over his schoolfellows at Harrow. He was a dunce. Because he was a dunce, his masters kept him in the lowest form until, by constant repetition, they ground into him a thorough and permanent grasp of English grammar. He never forgot the basic elements and used them all his life.

Many young businessmen and women, in their haste, snatch the basics of management techniques at the bottom of the ladder and then forget them half way up. Worse still, some fundamental skills essential to success are not even on offer. For instance, the techniques required for effective meetings rarely feature in the curriculum at universities. Even some business schools pay them scant regard. The oil tycoon, John D. Rockefeller, is often quoted as saying:

> The ability to deal with people is as purchasable a commodity as sugar and coffee, and I pay more for that ability than for any under the sun.

Few people would be prepared to dispute that truth.

It is said that two things in life are inevitable – death and taxes. We can add a third for anyone in business – meetings. A survey of more than 1000 hard-working managers revealed that meetings trouble them as much as any other aspect of their jobs. Meetings make the world go round. If there were no lovers' meetings, procreation would cease, birds would no longer sing and the human production line would grind to a halt. But we are not concerned here with such an awesome thought. We have enough problems with business meetings, which seem to dominate most of our working lives. Most managers would echo Harry's cry: 'In my job, life seems to be a series of eternal meetings, and most of them a complete waste of time. Help, please, help.'

'He's at a meeting.' How often does that response to your call frustrate your wish to do business with someone, especially as a customer? It seems that at any given time half the working world is at a meeting. But are the participants at work or merely at a meeting? Meetings that produce no profit, waste time and money. They also diminish all who take part in them. They can become just a necessary nuisance or, sometimes, even joyrides for those to whom meetings, at someone else's expense, are an easy-going way of life: anywhere they'd rather be than at work. Such odd creatures do exist, cluttering up meetings all over the world. If meetings represent the bloodstream of business, these people form thrombi – clots – that gum up the works. Could you be such a thrombus? Or are you the one in a hundred who takes meetings seriously and has devoted some thought and energy to equip himself to make his meetings productive? Of course you are that one in a hundred. You show your interest in meetings by handling this book for more than ten seconds. Happy to meet you.

At once, may I ask female readers to forgive the use of masculine words such as 'man', 'manager', 'him', 'his' and 'chairman' throughout? We could use him/her, manager/ess, or some similar devices; but that would become tedious. Please understand. Anyone who believes that women can be dismissed as nothing more than dainty ornaments in the rugged male world of business is a fool. Let us ignore him.

You will probably agree, ladies and gentlemen, that half a lifetime spent at dud meetings is really a slow death. It is within your power to refuse to accept such a fate. Your time is finite. Make the most of it. Determine that every meeting you attend is so much better because you are there, and not a complete waste of time – not your time anyway: and never a waste of your customers' time.

Why do we need meetings at all?

The main reason is because no business can exist as a one-man band. The fact that a business must have customers destroys the notion that anyone can go it alone. Other people always need to be considered and their needs satisfied – with customers at the top of the list. Even such soloists as actors, writers and artists of all sorts, who live to please, must also please to live. Many years ago this point was brought home to me by J. B. Priestley. I met the great man on Waterloo Station a few days after the first night of a new play of his.

'How's the play going?' I asked.

'It's not', he replied. 'It's gone. It's a flop.'

I offered my commiserations, but he stopped me with a low Yorkshire growl.

'I don't deserve sympathy. I wrote the thing to please myself. Should have known better. Take my tip, young Bell: never please yourself at the expense of the customer. Failure can be a lonely business. Avoid ego trips that separate you from other folk. That way leads to disaster!'

Can we eliminate meetings altogether? The answer must be 'No'. Primarily, we need meetings because we need customers. If we do not take the trouble to meet them and to understand their problems and how we can help them to solve those problems, someone else will do so and get the business. Customers. It is right that we should start with customers – all other people are only relative in importance. Successful business is about successful customers and the repeat orders they give you because you assist their success. If your customers fail, so do you. Should you not be acutely interested in your customers and what you can best do for them you are in the wrong job.

The sales people are at the sharp end in the front line. If the sales people cannot meet the customer and know his needs, if the design specialists do not discuss with the sales and production departments the practical aspects of the market requirements and if money matters are left to chance, chaos will result. We all depend on sharing expertise with other people. Even the experts need help.

Meetings vary as much as life itself. They range from a one-to-one job interview to Parliament; from a cricket team selection committee to the Trades Union Congress; from a half-empty church service to Billy Graham filling Wembley Stadium; from a routine board meeting to the Annual General Meeting of shareholders; from the Privy Council to the Old Bailey. Kings, queens, emperors and presidents meet. So do apprentices, members of Women's Institutes, bookies and barristers.

We must accept that meetings are necessary, but to be effective they must be more than a mere congregation of bodies: minds, knowledge and experience and clear objectives must also join forces.

When asked recently about meetings, conferences, seminars and other such gatherings, a director replied: 'Meetings? If I didn't watch out I'd spend so much time talking about business that I'd have no time left to do any!' Let us be quite clear from the start. The purpose of a business meeting is to get some action going towards better business. Discussion by all means, decisions certainly, but above all meetings must be made to pay for themselves and the outcome of a meeting should be action for business.

Talk is not cheap. Surprisingly few companies take the trouble to find out the cost-effectiveness – even the cost – of their meetings. A detailed investigation of several organizations revealed figures that astounded – in two cases shocked – senior management out of their delusion that good meetings just happen. In considering meetings we are in the realm of hard cash, often millions of pounds sterling, and dollars by the ton. 'Exaggeration' murmurs a dozy one.

Before cynics cry 'exaggeration', let them look into the facts. Let them find out with a detailed investigation what the company gets for its expenditure on meetings. Has anybody bothered to do this in your organization? The question is worth repeating. Have you or anybody else in your organization ever made a serious survey and a detailed investigation into the cost and cost-effectiveness of your meetings? If the answer is 'No', think about it.

If a workforce sits on its bottom with nothing to do, that is serious. If materials lose their value because they have been exposed to bad weather, bad workmanship or sheer waste, that is serious. Slack stock control, strikes, customers going elsewhere – all such deficiencies cost money, and the losses can be measured in terms of cash. But few companies consider the gaping hole in the moneybag caused by dud meetings. Few companies even know the price of their meetings or recognize it as a major cost.

Let us define a business meeting as two or more people getting together for a specific business purpose.

If you were to ask a group of managers to list all the meetings that occur in any large organization, their own perhaps, the result would run into hundreds of events – board meetings, management meetings of many sorts, production meetings, personnel interviews, sales interviews, union meetings, conferences, training, foreign trips, technical meetings, scientific research seminars, progress meetings – just to start with. Many more will occur to you.

Now consider the cost. Managers, directors and staff all cost money, even when they sit bored stiff and inactive at meetings. Fees and salaries; rail fares, air fares, hotel bills, expenses, cars, conference rooms, training premises (including rent, rates, heating, lighting and cleaning); secretarial preparation and the work of, say, accountants and others; literature, reports, handouts, etc. Companies who have been wise enough to study the expense of their meetings are usually aghast when confronted with the facts. After an in-depth survey one Norwegian company estimated the cost of its meetings at one and a quarter times its gross profit. A British giant quoted 'about £1 million a week' as its figure.

How can any sensible management afford to be casual about meetings? Apart from all the money thrown away, fruitless meetings erode and devalue the participants. They are more than a waste of time. They are a waste of life.

Any meetings that you attend should be the better for your presence. No meeting that you organize should be less than businesslike. We measure the success of a meeting by the profitable action that ensues. Be positive in your attitude towards meetings. In general, never call a meeting just to obtain a decision. Call your meetings to discuss, to decide and, if you decide on action, to get profitable action actually started as a result. The meeting will use up less time if the preparation has been thorough. More meetings fail through skimped preparation than for any other reason. The time occupied by a meeting is usually in inverse proportion to the length and depth of its preparation – the effectiveness of a meeting directly proportionate.

There is nothing unusual in this concept. A concert pianist delighting us with a performance of, say, Rachmaninov's Piano Concerto No. 2, probably spends eight hours a day practising. We get the impression that he has mastered all the difficulties of the work and that the performance is easy for him. In fact it is easy for him. The maestro has done his homework. If you add to this rehearsals and the accumulated years of study and practice undergone by the conductor, the leader, plus an orchestra of seventy other professional musicians you will realize that this enchanting evening has not just happened by chance – there has been a century or so of disciplined slog behind its creation.

A competitor in a championship golf tournament failed to beat the course record because he took five strokes at a par four hole. He was not due to play the next round until the following afternoon. He would have liked to get in some practice on that hole but the tournament rules forbade such a proceeding. At a nearby course he and his caddy roped and staked out a replica of the offending hole. They spent the entire morning working on it. In the afternoon the golfer got his par on the real thing – easily.

Good meetings are easy, too, so long as you know what you are about beforehand. Why should a businessman be less professional than a golfer or a musician? Be a professional meeting man – be prepared.

3   Before the meeting

Most people dislike long lists of do's and don't's. The Ten Commandments should suffice: but even these ancient bases of the good life have been misinterpreted, stretched, twisted and generally mauled to suit bigotry and self-interest. Precepts lose power as they multiply. Also, we tend to observe only those that fit our own way of life. If a dozen men and women were asked to start from scratch and to compose their own set of guidelines for mankind, a dozen different versions would ensu , reflecting each individual's own needs, experiences and hopes. An ice-cream salesman doing a roaring trade on a hot Sunday has not the same view of the Sabbath as a Free Presbyterian in the Western Isles. The restraints imposed on the General Synod of the Church of England might not apply to a routine meeting of shop stewards.

So, no absolute rules. No long lists.

As we are producing guidelines for your meetings – to suit your particular needs – you would, naturally, wish to discuss them, to consider them and to take a hand in their creation. You might be the big boss and able to delegate such matters. You might have to sort them out for yourself: or even for your boss. Good standards have more power and greater validity if they have gone through the filter of your own mind. Please join me at a meeting. Let us examine together a short case study. Pick out the errors for yourself. Then establish headings in note form. Later, we will consolidate them into your set of guidelines. Be positive. Turn all the faults that occur to you into what to do to avoid them. Have a paper and pencil handy.

What follows is an honest report of a so-called business meeting, plus a few explanatory notes. The names, only, are fictitious. The rest actually happened. You are, at this stage, looking for points to consider before a meeting.

John Dalton read the memo several times. It said:

From: J. B. Fishbourne (Chairman and Chief Executive)
To: John Dalton   Friday 2 September
The management meeting scheduled for Thursday September 15th has been brought forward to Tuesday the 6th. It will be held at Newport instead of HQ. Start at 0900 sharp.

No reason was given for the change. Dalton had appointments with customers on Tuesday the 6th. Also, he knew several towns called Newport in the UK – which one? Other difficulties arose so he decided to telephone Head Office for more information. The conversation went thus:

A female voice:'Hello.'
Dalton: 'Is that Fishbourne & Hawkes? (He needed to ask.)'
FV: 'Yes.'
Dalton: 'It's John Dalton here.'
FV: 'Who?'
Dalton: 'John Dalton, Sales Manager, Northern Division.'
FV: 'Yes.'
Dalton: 'May I speak to Mrs Carter, please?'
FV: 'Who?'
Dalton: 'Mrs Carter, Mr Fishbourne's secretary.'
FV: 'Oh, her. She's gone. Had a flaming row with Jimmy and left.'
Dalton: 'But she's only been there about six weeks.'
FV: 'Well she's not here any more.'
Dalton: 'Oh. I see. Who am I speaking to, please?'
FV: 'My name's Fiona and I'm Jimmy's new personal assistant. I don't like being called a secretary. Jimmy's a friend of my father so he'd better not try any hanky panky with me.'
Dalton: 'Of course not.'
                  (A pause)
FV: 'Did you want something?'
Dalton: 'Yes. I got a memo about the September

	management meeting. It's been changed from the 15th to the 6th.'
FV:	'I know that. I wrote the memo myself. What's wrong with it?'
Dalton:	'Could you give me a little more information please. For instance, where is the meeting being held?'
FV:	'The memo says quite clearly – Newport.'
Dalton:	'But which Newport? Newport, Gwent? Newport, Isle of Wight? Newport Pagnell? Newport – ?'
FV:	'It's the Newport in Essex.'
Dalton:	'I didn't know there was one.'
FV:	'It's the Newport near where Jimmy lives. That should be obvious.'
Dalton:	'I've never been to Mr Fishbourne's house. Is the meeting being held there?'
FV:	'No. He's got people staying. It's at the Pennington Conference Centre, about ten minutes away.'
Dalton:	'Have you sent us a road map?'
FV:	'There's no time for that now.'
Dalton:	'I see. We shall have to explore, shan't we?'
FV:	'Suit yourself.'
Dalton:	'The management meetings normally start at 1130 and go on after lunch. The memo says this one has a 0900 start.'
FV:	'So what?'
Dalton:	'Several of us have to travel quite a distance. For instance, I come from Middlesborough. A nine o'clock start means that I've got to travel on Monday, lose half a day's work and stay overnight.'
FV:	'Well?'
Dalton:	'Have you fixed accommodation? Do we stay at the conference centre?'
FV:	'You're free to make your own arrangements.'
Dalton:	'But why the nine o'clock start?'
FV:	'You know perfectly well – or you should do – that we're all going on to a race meeting. Jimmy

	has taken a box and a hospitality marquee. We're entertaining about a hundred guests.'
Dalton:	'Customers? Potential customers?'
FV:	'No, they're nearly all local – important people; friends of Jimmy's.'
Dalton:	'Pity. I've got two or three customers and prospects who would have enjoyed a day at the races.'
FV:	'Well your name's not on the list but I don't suppose Jimmy will mind your joining in.'
Dalton:	'Thanks. But what about the management meeting? What's the agenda?'
FV:	'As far as I can see there are only two main items to discuss. Mr Jackson's report on the European Potential for the next five years – '
Dalton:	'I haven't seen it yet.'
FV:	'The report's about fifty pages long and very boring. You'll get a copy when you arrive at the meeting, and the minutes of the last meeting, and the agenda – if they're ready in time. Also Jimmy says he wants to talk about the achievement of greater customer awareness. Satisfied?'
Dalton:	(with a sigh) 'Thank you very much.' (He hangs up.)'

You will infer that Fishbourne & Hawkes have management problems not confined to their meetings. At the end of this chapter turn to Appendix 1, page 109, which will help you to understand how they got into such disastrous straits. Not now, please: read it later. Let us concentrate now on the Dalton–Fiona conversation. Your own reactions to it are important. Draw from it points about what should be done before a meeting – preferably before you read on.

This Fishbourne and Hawkes management meeting is doomed to failure. The participants have been put to much annoyance and unnecessary work. They or their staff must find the location, find accommodation. All the nearby hotels are crammed with racegoers and people taking part in other conferences at the Pennington Centre. John Dalton settled for a pub twelve miles from Newport. At 0845 he arrived at the conference venue, in no mood for teamwork. The other nine managers, equally soured, aggregated their tales of woe into a solid lump of discontent. Because the booking had been made at the last minute, their meeting room was a makeshift – obviously a bedroom, not very well camouflaged. Fiona, of course, arrived late saying that Jimmy wouldn't be long. The managers eventually got themselves a cup of coffee and hung around. One of them suggested that in the meantime they might take a look at Jackson's report and study the agenda. Fiona giggled, 'Oh, they're all in Jimmy's car.'

At eighteen minutes to ten, Mr James Fishbourne swept into the room, greeted nobody, pushed himself into a chair and snapped. 'Come on let's get started. We're late. Get a move on. Sit down. We haven't got all day.'

The managers sat.

'Well, I suppose we'd better start with Jackson's report,' said Mr Fishbourne. He looked around.

'Where's Jackson?'

'I think he's in Edinburgh today,' murmured one of the managers with a hint of malice in his voice. 'Perhaps nobody told him that he was expected to make a presentation.'

Mr Fishbourne exploded. 'Oh, Christ! Can't I get any cooperation? Fiona, why isn't Jackson here?'

Fiona responded, bleakly, 'Well, he's not a manager. He's only a market researcher and I didn't think he'd be. . . .'

'Oh, never mind' interjected Mr Fishbourne. 'He's in your department, Swanson. Perhaps you'd better run through the report with us. Have you all read it?'

Three managers chorused, 'We haven't even seen it yet.'

A hiatus followed during which Fiona, with two grinning managers, hoisted the documents from the car outside and distributed them to the group.

The telephone rang. Fiona answered it. 'It's for you, Jimmy,' she said.

As is usual when a telephone is allowed to interrupt a meeting, everybody pretended to be uninterested, but in fact eagerly listened to every word, especially as the conversation appeared to be on a private matter. Mr Fishbourne's manner changed dramatically. The rasping voice became an oily purr. Obviously speaking to someone he considered important he switched on what he called his charm (he was known throughout the county as 'Prince Smarming'). The grovelling lasted, perhaps, five minutes. Mr Fishbourne replaced the receiver.

'That was Lord Buttridge,' he remarked loftily. 'A pal of mine.'

The managers were not impressed. A silence ensued.

'Well, we'd better get on with the report. Swanson – where's Swanson? Where the hell's Swanson?'

John Dalton said, 'He needs an overhead projector, a screen and video equipment. He's trying to rustle them up from somewhere. Perhaps while we're waiting we could get on with the next item on the agenda. I gather you want to discuss greater customer awareness – that was it, wasn't it?'

But the meeting never got around to the achievement of greater customer awareness. Nor was Jackson's report discussed. Twelve noon inexorably arrived and the races called. Mr Fishbourne answered the call. Ten sickened managers departed to continue their ongoing search for another job.

Positive thinking and planning lead to constructive and cost-effective meetings.

Successful meetings result from intelligent preparation by:

1   The organizer
2   The Chairman
3   The members

The preliminaries set the atmosphere for success. The birth of a child can only be the triumph that Nature intended it to be if the conception and the pregnancy have been well managed. You will already have in your notes that everything that can be done in advance to ensure a good meeting will be done.

4   Organizing a meeting

In a ship of the Royal Navy, the nearest thing to God is the Captain. He is held in awe by the ratings who rarely see him. When the ship is first commissioned, the order 'Clear lower decks' rings out and all hands are mustered to listen to the great man. His speech nearly always includes the phrase: '. . . and an efficient ship is a happy ship.' This oration is, of course, known on the lower deck as the fish and chip speech. Having delivered this great truth (and it is true that people are happier working in a well-run organization than trying to cope with a mess) the Captain disappears somewhere aft to leave the day-to-day running of the ship to his First Lieutenant, dubbed 'Jimmy the One'. The Captain takes full responsibility. His Number One gets the work done. They must know and respect each other's minds. As a result of their excellent training and experience they are able to agree on routine matters. They confer frequently to keep information flowing both ways to meet the changing needs of every new situation. An efficient ship is a happy ship.

In the business world one of the marks of a first-class manager is a clear desk. He seems to have little to do and plenty of time in which to do it. He has, of course, chosen his staff with great care and trained them if necessary. He delegates, trusts them to get on with the job and supports them. He has decided that a meeting is necessary. Put yourself in the position of someone who has been asked by such a manager to organize the meeting. Regard yourself as his First Lieutenant. If you are experienced, most of the steps you now take will be routine – standard practices established by you and the manager over many effective meetings. Or are you a tyro in pastures new? Whatever your status, you must match your thinking to that of your chief. Discuss fully and get your briefing crystal clear. You and he must work together, plan meticulously and coordinate every move to make the meeting successful. Where the borders are between what you do and what he does will, of course, vary with each relationship. What? Why? Who? How? Where? and When? questions are proven starters for discussions of this sort. If you have not already done so, establish between you good working routines and fill in the details for each meeting.

To ensure that nothing is overlooked, you should create and use a checklist and see to it that your chief also uses one. Do not scorn memory-joggers. The best people rely on them. When one is flying it is a comfort to know that everything has been checked and double checked before take-off. Even the most experienced of aircrews use an aide memoire. A submarine commander does not give the order to dive without knowing that all watertight doors are closed and that numerous other routines are carried out, and checked, and double checked. (You may recall a recent marine disaster caused by the failure to ensure that all doors were firmly shut before departure. The calamity would not have happened had a checklist and corroborating signals been in operation.)

Your checklist might not necessarily be the same as, say, a Company Secretary's who has obligatory legal factors to consider. It is your checklist that we are working on. We must, perforce, generalize here and ask you to omit or add points to suit your own circumstances. However, some matters are of fundamental importance for any meeting and these we will note – we are looking at the preliminaries, laying foundations.

Ask yourself: Are you completely clear about the purpose of the meeting? What business is it intended to achieve? Specify and define the scope, the limitations within which the meeting will operate. For example, are you seeking a decision about extra pay for weekend working or discussing the pay structure of the entire workforce? Meetings drift into irrelevancies unless firm targets have been established and recognized by the participants. You must be sufficiently clear about the objectives to be able to convey such information to all concerned.

Now that you have clarified the intended business of the meeting, the next job is to select and bring together the men and women who can best get the business done. Sometimes, as with a board of directors or a standing committee, the membership is already known. You might only have to consider whether extra people with specialized knowledge should be asked to help with a particular item on the agenda: for example Mr Jackson and his report.

Beware of a routine string of names, unedited for years. Avoid the non-contributors. There are thousands of such freeloaders adding weight to meetings but no substance. One example should suffice. The new head of a government department in the north of England found his budget too tight for comfort. With his secretary he examined, among other matters, the costs of departmental meetings. They uncovered one man, a Mr George Barrington, who for the past four years had been released from the department once each month to attend a regular meeting in London. They could find no reason for his presence at these meetings. The manager asked Mr Barrington for an explanation. Under pressure, it emerged that he had taken advantage of laxity on the part of his former manager and the convenors of the London meetings. Barrington had once been sent to represent the department on a special matter. He was now on the list of people attending and had been invited, monthly, ever since. The computer was made the scapegoat: the computer was said to be at fault for issuing subsequent invitations. Mr Barrington, a keen theatregoer and concert buff, saw something most attractive in being able to travel to London on Friday and stay with friends until Sunday evening when he occupied the hotel room supplied by the department. On Monday, he would join the eighteen or so others at the meeting, melt into the pool and, later, return north – all under the cover of an official summons and with departmental acquiescence, first-class travel and all expenses found. Mr Barrington doesn't do that any more. Invite the Jacksons and watch out for the Barringtons.

You now have a clear business purpose and you have the right people to get the business done. You have established two of the main foundations of a good meeting. Next, you must create the conditions within which they can work most effectively. The date, the time and the venue must be considered. Regular board meetings ought to be straightforward, but even boardrooms have been double booked before now by the Training Department or other management groups. All internal conference rooms should be subject to forward planning and reserved at one central point to prevent such a contretemps. Book your room well in advance.

For conferences outside your own premises it is advisable to inspect the venue before you book it. Is the size appropriate for your needs? Eight hundred people attending a performance at the Albert Hall look very thin on the ground, indicating a flop. Eight hundred people in the Old Vic represent a full house and a roaring success. The auditorium must be not too small, not too large but just right. This point is particularly important if someone is making a presentation.

For committee work, a cramped room with perhaps a dozen people competing for space around the table will help nobody. Will they also have to compete for air? Check the ventilation, especially if smoking is permitted. Lack of oxygen induces drowsiness, even before a liquid lunch. Treat the assertion that the place is air-conditioned with some reserve. Open a few windows. It is usually better to open two or three windows on one side of the room only than to have a gale blowing through. If open windows let in the roar of city traffic or the thump of a pile-driver on an adjacent building site, refuse to accept the room. I have a vivid recollection of attending a conference in a hotel at which we were expected to work against a Palm Court Orchestra – with only a heavy drapery separating us. An unsuitable environment in an ill-managed hotel is no place for your meeting. Go elsewhere. There are many excellent conference rooms with caring staffs. Get to know them. You will find it worthwhile.

Too large a room offers many distractions and people feel marooned in excessive space. Ideally, for a committee-type meeting, the table should provide ample elbow room (literally), free areas for documents, writing materials, samples and easily-reached soft drinks. The members should be able to move behind the chairs without bumping into the furniture or jabbing backs. Subdued boudoir lamplight is soporific. Check the lighting. Get it changed if necessary. Find out where all the switches are, especially if you are using equipment such as videos, overhead projectors or films. Can such things as screens and spotlights be easily positioned to suit the participants and the presenter? Make friends with the operator who maintains the equipment on site. He knows the place better than you do. Work with him and arrange for immediate contact with him should things go awry. You will, of course, install and test all props and equipment well before the meeting starts. Don't forget to have spare parts handy should, say, a light bulb in the projector fail. You are not being a fusspot: you are simply working as a professional.

If the meeting is likely to last more than two hours, organize clear breaks for refreshment. Have the coffee set, served and cleared away in an adjoining room, not at the conference table. Clear-cut intervals give the members a chance to stretch their legs, answer the call of nature, smoke outside, receive urgent messages and, if necessary, use a telephone – again, outside the room. There should not be a telephone in the room. Indicate in your joining instructions that there will be such breaks. Fifteen minutes should be enough. Restart promptly.

You want your members to feel welcome and important. Few things are more deflating than to arrive at the reception desk and to be met with a vacant stare from a receptionist who knows nothing about your meeting. If it is practicable, be in the lobby to greet your people, or appoint one of your staff to do so. At least ensure that the receptionist has a list of names and can steer the visitors to the conference room. Let them know where they can wash their hands. Check with them that you have spelt their namecard correctly and that they have received all the necessary documents. After a long journey a cup of something might be offered. Their presence has been requested. They have taken the trouble to arrive. Make them feel appreciated. They will work better if the atmosphere is cordial and businesslike from the start. You will feel better, too, with a few smiles around.

5 Paperwork

Now that your meeting has an agreed purpose, you have the right people and the right place, your next job is to draft – and to agree with your chief – the documentation.

Invitations and notices should be sent out neither so far in advance that they might be forgotten nor so late that members might have accepted conflicting appointments.

Your members will want to know where the meeting will be held and, if necessary, to receive detailed travel instructions. Suitable train times or other information such as parking arrangements are a help. So, too, are maps and road plans. Will they be met at the airport or the station? Have you fixed overnight accommodation for them? In an emergency they might need the telephone numbers of the venue and their hotel. Include the code. To tell them it's Leatherhead 60005 means that they have to look it up – not easy if one's car has conked out on a B road somewhere in the wilds. Let them know not only the time at which the meeting will start but also when it will end. Include information about breaks for refreshment – make it clear that these breaks are the only times for their telephone calls. Messages will be intercepted at the desk and handed to them at an appropriate interval.

What documents should your members study in advance? Reports, financial statements, architect's or engineering drawings, ground plans, etc. You must give your members every chance to be thoroughly prepared. To have them skimming an important document during the meeting, probably while somebody else is talking, is a poor substitute for studied consideration. Also prepare literature which might be more useful as handouts during the progress of the meeting if they are needed. Have namecards printed boldly so that they are easily readable from the far end of the table. For a larger meeting lapel badges may be substituted. Please do not merely type them so that one has to embrace the other fellow to find out who he is. Make them readable at two yards. On some occasions it would be useful to send to members a list of people who will be attending.

Have you made arrangements for the minutes to be taken? Do not inflict this task on a member of the meeting: this is a job for a neutral, not a participant – who would thus be neutered.

Some top people who chair many meetings ask their Number Ones to prepare a brief outlining the main facts of the situation. They frequently take charge of a meeting otherwise unarmed. You should never attempt this onerous task without complete understanding of his requirements. You are both responsible people. Be professional. Time spent in discussion and research pays great dividends. Off the cuff is never enough.

Chairman's brief

For a regular committee

1 Notes on handling (e.g. if there is a change in the agenda).
2 Notes on each item – a few lines only, summarizing:
   (a) The issue.
   (b) The objective.
   (c) Compromise positions.

For an ad hoc meeting

1 If needed, notes on key people attending, including their organizations, position, their special expertise, attitudes to issues.
2 Notes on each item:
   (a) Issue/background.
   (b) Line to take.
   (c) Strong points.
   (d) Defensive points.

If the meeting is very long and complex, the Chairman's brief can be in two parts:

1   A 'steering brief' – not more than two pages – which the Chairman can use *at* the meeting.
2   A separate page of notes on each item which the Chairman can use to prepare himself *before* the meeting.

You will, of course, make your Chairman aware of correspondence and other recent developments relevant to the issues to be discussed.

The agenda

Let us nod respectfully to the purist who insists that the word agenda – things to be done – is plural. Most people find it more convenient to use the word as a singular, meaning a list, a programme of the business for a meeting. Its object is to tell all those who should attend the subjects that will be discussed so that they can think about them beforehand. A well-planned agenda gives the meeting a disciplined shape. It also ensures that no item of importance is overlooked.

At, say, an Annual General Meeting of a public limited company, such items as: to adopt the report and accounts for the year; to declare a final dividend; to appoint directors and auditors; to authorize an amendment to the rules, will be encountered. We can safely leave the organization of legally-imposed meetings to the qualified Company Secretary. Amateurs dabble in legal matters at their peril.

At the other end of the scale, some informal meetings work without an agenda. But even casual meetings become more businesslike if, by telephone or letter, the members know, at least, what they will be dealing with.

Items for the agenda are collected from the minutes of the previous meeting, from relevant correspondence, from knowledge of current events, from the chairman, from the members. Do not encourage the members to expect you to chase them for items they wish to include. They should come to you and let you know. Please keep in mind that a meeting can only deal effectively with so much at any one time. Too much on one agenda could indicate that the group is not meeting often enough.

What follows is a typical agenda for a regular meeting of a working group:

1   Chairman's introduction – opening the meeting.
2   Apologies for absence.
3   Minutes of the last meeting.
4   Matters arising from the minutes.
5   Correspondence.
6   Reports.
7   Motions.
8   Date of the next meeting.
9   Any other business.
10 Close.

Item 1   Is discussed in Chapter 7.

Item 2   It is a discourtesy to the chair and to the other members not to let them know the reason for your absence.

Item 3   The minutes of the last meeting should have been circulated soon afterwards. The action section which details names and dates for specific people forms an integral part of the minutes. Everybody concerned should have received a copy of the minutes of the previous meeting, be expected to have read them, and to have acted upon them before arriving at this meeting. The alternative is for the secretary to read the minutes to the meeting. This can be a bore especially as he has other documents, such as correspondence, to put to the meeting. It also occupies time which could be used more productively. The chairman puts the question as to whether the minutes are acceptable. At some meetings, a proposer and seconder to: 'that the minutes be agreed' is normal. If they are approved the chairman signs them on behalf of the group. The secretary files copies of the minutes of all meetings in the minute book, thus keeping a complete record.

Item 4   This means exactly what it says. It does not mean that the minutes can be altered in any way – once they have been agreed and signed.

Item 5   The correspondence, which the secretary reads, usually provides information about developments since the previous meeting. Sometimes copies of correspondence are tabled for discussion.

Item 6　Reports would probably cover action taken or information lacking at the last meeting. These are usually read by the authors, but the secretary, again, might have to speak. Sometimes these reports will have been circulated beforehand or tabled at the meeting (more paperwork!).

Item 7　Motions – 'that such and such an action be taken'. Motions must always be presented in the affirmative and capable of being answered 'Yes' or 'No'.

Item 8　The date of the next meeting must be agreed and announced.

Item 9　Whether any other business can be permitted at the current meeting must be decided early on.

Item 10　Close.

As soon as the meeting has closed the chairman and the secretary should leave the room to avoid an unofficial meeting about the meeting, which often causes trouble.

Minutes

The task of writing the minutes can become slavery, without thanks, for the secretary. Minutes should be written as soon as possible, while the subjects are still fresh in the minds of both the secretary and the members. It is not unknown for members to ask the secretary to write what, on reflection, they wish they had said rather than the truth. You will of course not oblige them. The minutes are a brief but accurate account of the business transacted at the meeting.

The proceedings of the House of Commons are recorded verbatim. Massive volumes of Hansard contain millions of words – every pearl, every gaffe, every expletive, all the wisdom and all the nonsense spouted in the House. It will comfort you to know that such extravagance is not required for your minutes.

Legally, all you need to do is to record the decision: but that will not suffice for an efficient business organization. We need a permanent record of:

- A reference number, if the meeting is one of a series. (It would be time-saving for you in the writing to use

headings, some of which could be standard for a series of regular meetings.)
- Where and when the meeting was held.
- Who chaired the meeting.
- Who was present.
- Who was absent.
- A statement that the agenda was adhered to e.g. that the minutes of the previous meeting were agreed and signed, etc.
- A few lines summarizing reports. (Include their file numbers so that members can, if they wish, obtain copies.)
- A summary of any discussion that followed the reports.
- All motions and amendments in the exact form they were put by the chairman.
- The names of the mover (proposer) and seconder of each motion and amendment.
- A summary of the *main* points of the discussions.
- The numbers of those voting.
- The decision taken on each proposal.
- Who takes what action – and by when.
- The date of the next meeting.

   Keep in mind that you are not writing elegant fiction, but a simple record of what transpired. People who were unable to attend the meeting will need to be informed of the flavour of the meeting and the strength of voting opinion. Inform them. People who were present require you to confirm what they and their colleagues discussed and decided. Use an impersonal style. Try not to bruise egos. One device is to avoid naming the defeated. Record that such and such a view was put forward. Avoid dialogue or quoting long-winded speeches. Reduce rambling discussions to a clear statement of main points. Include the essentials but be ruthless about the garbage. Hours into minutes should be your watchword. But do remember that we might have to refer back to the minutes in case of a dispute, so please, no false economy.
   Many busy people prefer to have the substance of the minutes agreed on the spot. At the conclusion of each item, the chairman sums up the main pros and cons of the discussion; clearly states the decision reached; and delegates' action,

naming who does what and by when. The secretary takes note and reads back what the chairman has dictated. Usually the group will assent, without further discussion.

Post-meeting

A copy of the minutes, with an attached sheet emphasizing actions to be taken, should be sent to everybody who has a right and a need to know – as soon as possible. If the minutes are likely to be delayed, the action sheet should be sent separately, and at once.

It would be a discourtesy not to let the chairman have a sight of the minutes before they are issued. It would also be unwise: you might be in error.

One of the secrets of successful meetings is, first, to succeed in obtaining the precious gift of a first-class secretary.

6 Chairmanship – before the meeting think awhile

Power tends to corrupt, and absolute power corrupts absolutely. *Lord Acton (1834–1902)*

Power is the ability to insist on it. If you happen to be the boss, chairing a meeting, and you consistently get your way by asserting your power, there is no need for you to have meetings at all. Simply impose orders. But you cannot expect any future meeting that becomes necessary to be a gathering of devoted enthusiasts. There are more ways than one of killing a cat and there are better ways of getting what you want from a meeting than by saying, 'Don't bother me with your opinions. My mind is made up.' In great men there is, ever-present, a streak of humility.

But that does not mean that one needs to be spineless and unable to dominate when the occasion demands. Indeed, many of your meetings will be called only for one purpose – to instruct, to brief people about what you have already decided. So long as everyone is quite clear from the beginning that the meeting has no other objective, there should be no difficulty, especially if at some earlier meetings they have taken part in guiding you towards the decision to take such action.

People taking part is the operative phrase. Participants should feel at the end of your meeting that they have truly contributed something of value; that their knowledge, experience and needs have moved the meeting towards an excellent decision. If they have taken part in the decision, they will also undertake the ensuing action much more willingly than they will accept a mandatory order thrust upon them. A good chairman sees to it that his members participate, productively. He has power; but he also appreciates that his power is a trust and that he is accountable for the use he makes of it.

So, Mr Chairman, you are in charge. But what are you? Are you a sort of referee, an umpire, the keeper of the rule book;

the arbiter, the judge on the bench? You are all these things and more. You are also the stimulator, the mover-on, the helmsman, the captain, the diplomat, the clarifier, the pacifier, the mopper-up of tears and the common friend to all. But essentially and most importantly you are a businessman and your chief function is to achieve the business of the meeting, in reasonable time, at a reasonable cost and with benefit to all concerned.

It might seem a little perverse, but from the outset – long before the meeting starts – you must have in your mind what profitable action should result from the meeting. Who should do what? And why? What could be the perfect solution to the problem in hand? If the perfect answer is not feasible, what other options are there? What is the nearest you could get to the optimum? The meeting itself forms only one link in a chain of events. If the other links lack strength the meeting can become merely the place where the chain breaks. Ninety per cent of an effective meeting happens before the meeting starts. Forging the before-the-meeting link requires thought, horse sense and skill. If you intend to call a meeting, be completely clear about its intended purpose. What specific business should the meeting achieve? Is it to decide on action, to brief people, to inform, to persuade? What in specific terms – no vague abstractions – is the business purpose of the meeting? You must then face what might be a deflating question: Is a meeting necessary at all? Must you deprive people of their time and put the company to expense? Can the business be done – the decision made – in some other way – a few telephone calls, perhaps, or half a dozen letters? Why are you proposing to call the meeting? Why? Any one of us could live comfortably on the costs of meetings that are held every Tuesday for no other reason than that a meeting is held every Tuesday. Your meeting, of course, is not one of those. Are you sure? Is there a solid business reason for your meeting? It's worth asking.

So you decide that your meeting is a necessity; the business cannot be accomplished without a combination of other minds, interests and experience. Which people can provide you with such a combination? Nobody else should be invited. You want to get some business done. Avoid the hangers-on and the strange creatures who go to meetings just to get out of their own offices for a while. If your business is to get a decision and action, beware of the second-string man who cannot give a firm yes or no. He has to report back to his boss. Then there will have to be another meeting for his boss or even his boss's boss. Invite and accept only the people who can do the job properly. Do not forget, as so often happens, to invite the man who will have to take any action you decide upon. If your meeting decides to change the production line you cannot expect joyous cooperation from the production manager who was elsewhere when you decided how to run his department. Also, it might be of greater value to ask a junior who has, for instance, done the research to present his findings rather than have his manager present them second hand. Remember Jackson and his report.

When and where the meeting takes place depends on the urgency of the business and the convenience of the people concerned. Be considerate about this. Merely the fact that you operate from Edinburgh does not necessarily mean that your Brighton and Cardiff colleagues will agree that your office is the perfect location. Must you start your meeting at 0900, which means an overnight trip for everyone except you? Sensibly arranging the date, the hour and the location can show you to be a thoughtful organizer.

On the other hand, I know of one director who calls his department heads to a meeting every Friday, at 1520, sharp. They get through an astonishing amount of work by 1700. This practice has its points. The members come prepared, knowing that, otherwise, they will be steamrollered and swept aside. These meetings get down to brass tacks without delay, and uninformed waffle gets short shrift. The main drawback is that action arising out of a Friday meeting loses immediacy because nothing gets done over the weekend. A cold engine on a Monday morning is not the perfect start to the week however enthusiastic one was on Friday. Nevertheless, if your regular meetings tend to drag on, you might like to consider a limited season of such short, sharp meetings to revitalise the doodlers and the lax. Should you wish immediate action, the day need not be a Friday.

If your colleagues have to examine reports, plans, figures or must equip themselves in other ways in preparation for the meeting, give them a fair chance to do so. Also, make clear to them precisely what the business of the meeting will be and that you expect them to come prepared. A meeting that has to be recalled because relevant facts and key people are missing reflects no credit on the convenor or the members. More meetings fail because the preparation has been neglected or skimped than for any other reason. No one should go to a meeting ill-prepared. Even if the meeting happens to be a quick get-together, and at short notice, a few minutes' thought beforehand will increase your value as a meetingman. At least one member, you, will be able to talk sense.

Ask yourself a few questions and try not to evade them until you have clear answers. For example:

1   What is the precise objective of the meeting?
2   Exactly what is the subject of the discussion and what are the limits within which this meeting will work. Define the scope, now, or else the meeting might ramble into a maze of useless byways – possibly connected with the subject but irrelevant to the objective.
3   Having pinned down the purpose, the subject and the terms of reference, ask yourself: Is the meeting necessary at all? Can you make the decision unaided? Perhaps you can, but is that desirable? Would you get as much cooperation with the subsequent action if your colleagues took no part in the decision? Also, you could be in error. They may have experience and facts which bring a new light to the problem. A wise man is always ready to change his mind in the face of facts.

Meetings proliferate in some organizations for a variety of dodgy reasons. An unworthy chairman will sometimes call a meeting because he wishes to avoid responsibility should things go wrong. 'The committee took the decision: it wasn't my fault.' He will, of course, grab the credit if things should go right. An unworthy chairman often calls a meeting to show that he can order people about and to confirm his boss-status. Poor, deluded chap. He forgets that status is based on what other people think of us, not what we think of ourselves:

O wad some pow'r the giftie gie us
To see ourselves as others see us!

It wad frae mony a blunder free us
and foolish notion.
>   *Robert Burns (To a mouse)*

You will wish to lead from the front, by example. Any deficiencies you have weaken your influence. They must be recognized honestly and replaced by strengths. You are much like the leader of an expedition. Obviously, you must know where you are going, and why. You must know the terrain. You must know your colleagues. You must plan the route and stake out the main staging posts. You must establish agreed rules of procedure and behaviour. You must create controls. In fact you must be ready for anything.

'After the ball was over' is too late for dancing lessons: it would be wiser to take them beforehand.

Too late. Too late. (A short fable)

Long, long ago in a lonely village far beyond the backwoods, there lived a simple man called Twerpus. He was making ready to visit the distant market. As he backed his horse between the shafts of his wagon, a travelling salesman, one Spiv, accosted him saying, 'Wherefore dost thou use a horse to draw thy wagon? I have here a cart propelled by an engine which possesses the power of twenty horses. Allow me to offer thee a free demonstration. No obligation, of course.'

Spiv pushed a knob, pulled a lever and – lo! – the horseless cart moved forward twenty leg-lengths. Then Spiv pulled where he had pushed and pushed where he had pulled, thus stopping the cart. The eyes of Twerpus grew large with desire.

'What cost must I pay,' he cried 'to possess this marvel?'

Quoth Spiv: 'I would not part from this marvel: but, to thee, as a special favour I will accept the sheep that thou hast already loaded plus fifty spondulicks and the wagon and horse in part exchange.'

'Agreed,' replied Twerpus. ('Tis said that every minute a sucker is born.)

Seemingly testing the horse for speed, Spiv and the wagon rapidly vanished over the horizon and Twerpus, agog with joy, called, 'Wife! Come hither! I have a horseless cart to carry us to the market!'

'How can a cart move without a horse?' enquired Maria, his wife.

'Observe,' chuckled Twerpus 'I push this knob and I pull this lever, thus.'

The cart moved forward a few leg-lengths then smote a tree with a mightly thwack.

'Idiot!' shouted Maria. 'Why didst thou not pull the right hand rein or the left hand rein to steer the cart away from the tree?'

Twerpus gazed at the damaged cart, perplexed.

'Alas,' he said 'there is no right hand rein, neither is there left. There is no steering control at all.'

Maria snorted: 'Thou shouldst have thought of that before.'

'Bring me ropes,' demanded Twerpus. 'One shall pull the wheel towards the left and the other to the right.'

The ropes were made fast. Twerpus once more started the engine and steered the cart around some trees.

'Lo and behold, oh my wife, a control is now to my hand.'

'Aye,' replied Maria 'but lo and behold the ruin thou hast brought to the cart. Thou shouldst have thought of controls before.'

Twerpus paid no heed. 'Let us together go to the market. Load more sheep, wife, and enter into the cart thyself.'

That done, Twerpus pushed the knob and pulled the lever. The cart staggered forward. All went merry as a marriage bell until the going down of a hill. The cart gathered speed. Twerpus pulled the knob and pushed the lever as hard as he could push and pull, but nothing would stop the cart until it smote another tree – with an even mightier thwack.

'Idiot,' screamed Maria with the voice of a thousand jays. 'No brakes! No brakes! Thou shouldst have thought of brakes before, before, before – tis now too late. . . .'

You do not need any more of this fable: but you do get the point that only a Twerpus leaves considerations of control until matters get out of hand. Now, not later, is the time to arm yourself with the means to control your meeting. Let us muster the supporters you already have, briefly review them and enlist more to add to your strength. As a successful manager, you work with an efficient Number One who will handle many of the practical details and take an equal pride with you that your meetings are business meetings – always. You cannot show such a treasure too much appreciation so long as it does not descend into soft soap. We all like a deserved pat on the back. (If your Number One is a dud it's probably your fault. We usually get the staff we deserve. Do something about it.)

You will have agreed between you matters of routine: but keep even the routines on your checklists. Discuss every meeting. Sometimes this will require only a few minutes, sometimes longer.

Let us look at your strengths, so far:

Strength One: Your First Lieutenant.

Strength Two: You have the objective of the meeting crystal clear and have invited only suitable people to help you to achieve it. You have developed a genuine interest in your members, are well aware of their expertise and have considered their quirks, their likely attitudes, their problems and their needs.

Strength Three: You have equipped yourself with sufficient knowledge of the subject under discussion to be able to ask intelligent questions. You must not pose as an expert but you need to know enough about the subject to avoid looking stupid. Check your briefing and ask questions, beforehand, about anything unclear. Scan the documents. Be, at least, an informed layman.

Now is the time to plan the structure of your meeting and to organize your control points. The prime requirement is that you and your members have in common a respect for each other. One cannot demand respect: it can only be earned – usually by giving it in full measure to the other fellow. Flattery is insulting but genuine appreciation of a man's true values warms the cockles of his heart. Emerson wrote:

> Every man I meet is superior to me in some way – and from him I can learn.

Of course your members bring knowledge and experience that you lack. Otherwise they are unnecessary at your meeting. But, like you, they are not angels: neither are they infallible. People willingly observe rules and formalities so long as they make sense for the particular occasion and are clearly laid down and agreed from the start.

You have probably had enough of theory for a while and would prefer a little action. Please join me at a meeting at which we will test the controls already discussed and sketch in a few more. You are in the chair. GB (the author) will interpolate comments from time to time.

May we assume for the moment that your meeting is not a grand affair but the sort of event that businessmen and women enjoy or endure almost every day? It is due to start at 0900.

7   Those present at your meeting

1   The Managing Director. You know about yourself but, for the purpose of this exercise, may we call you Andrew Scott? You are 46 years old and became MD seven years ago.
2   Alan Thompson, 42, Financial Director. A chartered accountant. Strictly a money man who would have been better equipped had he also received some training along the lines of a chartered company secretary. A good chap but not fully rounded. He has worked on the new factory venture with enthusiasm and great skill. For you, a supporter, a plus.
3   Jack Dawson, 54, Production Director. A qualified engineer, has been with the firm twenty-three years. A solid citizen and a leading influence in local society and sports organizations. He has already rejected the suggestion that he move house to run the new factory. You anticipate that he will repeat his proposal that the factory be located nearer to the existing one so that he can more readily oversee both: otherwise, a supporter.
4   Tony Sharp, 38, Sales Director. A real ball of fire. Somewhat brash but he gets results. His contract enables him to earn more than any other director. Apt to chase rainbows but listens to you, whom he admires. You have earlier spotted his potential, groomed him and promoted him from the ranks. He is not a yes man: neither would you wish him to be.
5   Lucinda Carson, 50, Personnel Director. A high-born, well-educated collar-and-tie woman. Brilliant. In the wake of a disastrous strike two years ago, she was brought into the firm at board level to restructure the 'Human Resources' aspect of the business. Everybody likes Lucinda (one dare not call her Linda or Cindy). a

tremendous asset despite occasional bias. Frequently clashes with the labour relations manager – and usually wins. She will probably ride a pet hobby horse. You must have a snaffle ready.

At sub-board level:

6   John Betts, 48, Works Manager. A competent square peg in a snug-fitting square hole. You have privately considered transferring him to the new plant and promoting him to the board: but John lacks self-control and other OLQs (officer-like qualities). He's better where he is now; loyal and doing a good job under Jack Dawson.

7   Robert (Bob) Lockyer, 52, Labour Relations Manager. Started work thirty-eight years ago as an apprentice in a heavy engineering plant. Yours is his fourth company. Hard working, self-educated. With the help of the excellent trades union training he has become an authority within his sphere. He can quote trade union law as accurately as most people can say the Lord's Prayer. Bob's attitude to the management is still *them* and *us*: but he makes the mind of the workforce clear to you. You rightly regard him as an asset.

8   Graham Todd, 40, Administration and Estates Manager. Trained as an architect: has worked as a government official and knows the ropes within official circles. A stickler for detail. Thoroughly reliable but he is a loner, shy, needs drawing out.

9   Albert Fox, 54, Transport Manager. Family man with five children – all girls. Thorough knowledge of his job, which he does very well indeed. Has occasional flashes of wry humour.

10   Mrs Margaret Martin, 46, your secretary. Count your blessings. You are a lucky man.

You arrived at your office at 0800 and have cleared matters needing immediate attention. Maggie (Mrs Martin) has prepared a brief and you have run through it with her. She leaves to check that everything is set for the meeting and that coffee is ready to greet the members in a room alongside the boardroom. (Detail: John Betts prefers a cup of strong tea, Lucinda Carson, mineral water. Detail attended to.) The

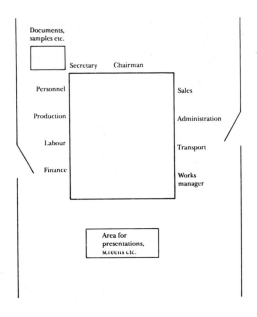

Figure 1

members know each other. You are on first name terms with
all of them: the reverse is not necessarily so. Your colleagues
have been conditioned to arrive ten minutes or so before
meetings. They know that this meeting, without any interval,
will end at 1045 and that you are a stickler for a prompt,
businesslike start. You join them for a few minutes to
exchange greetings and take advantage of any opportunity to
improve the atmosphere. For example, you say to Albert Fox:
'How was the swimming gala last night? Did Millie do well?'
(You know that she did. Maggie gave you the news earlier.)
Albert glows with pride and answers: 'Aye, she did. She did
very well. Won by six lengths and broke the club record.'
There are smiles and congratulations all round and, in a mood
most agreeable, they follow you into the boardroom – with
maybe three minutes to spare.

Starting the meeting

A good chairman creates a team with a common aim, to get
the business done with the greatest profit for all concerned.

The profit need not be money, although that is usually the ultimate aim.

Effective speakers establish a good relationship with their audience at the outset. A chairman has the additional responsibility of establishing good relationships between the members of the meeting. The manner in which you begin can colour the entire proceedings.

Be the last to be seated. If you sit with egg on your face waiting for them, you have missed a trick. Have them seated ready to get to work. The moment your backside reaches the chair is an important moment. The effect should be that the meeting is now officially under way.

The group will respond to your manner at the start. If you casually loll in the chair and dither, that becomes the key attitude of the members towards the business in hand. Be firm, be pleasant, be businesslike. If introductions need to be made, make them. Briefly sketch in the background of the problem under discussion. Then, with a sure touch, build in the controls which will sustain your authority and help to keep the business moving at the right pace and in the right direction.

Remind the members of the exact purpose of the meeting. Declare the scope and the limits within which this subject is meant to be explored at this meeting. If, later on, someone with an axe to grind strays outside these limits you have a legitimate choke chain with which to pull him back into line. Discourage time wasters, now. Remind everyone that the meeting and its members have a time limit. Also discourage the prima donnas. Make it clear that every member of the meeting is important, and that we want their views: that is why they were invited.

Get the nod from the members about these control points at the start. They will sound arbitrary if you try to impose them later.

So now your meeting has a clear, common objective. The scope and limits are specific. Every member knows that his contribution is needed. They are aware that time is finite and valuable. They realize that the chairman knows what he is about and is worthy of their respect.

The larger the meeting, the greater the need for formalities. Even a small gathering works better within suitable rules. Get these agreed at the start. To make them up as you go along just does not work.

If someone is making a formal presentation for discussion, decide and announce beforehand whether questions will be permitted during the presentation or left until the end. Otherwise matters could get out of hand.

After a moment to allow them to settle down, you take the chair. The meeting has begun. Your opening remarks should establish the firm framework within which the meeting will work. Also your control points must not only be made clear but also accepted by the group, now. The style and the language you use will obviously be yours, not mine, but may I suggest something like the following:

You look agreeable, glance at the clock and say: 'Nine o'clock. Good. Let's start. Thank you very much for being on time. We have a lot of business to do. Some of you have other appointments after the meeting so we must finish by 1045.'

Control point: Time. You might need to use time to check the garrulous and the gossipy. Also as a prod to stimulate progress towards decisions. In your preparation you have allocated time allowances for each item and will keep an eye on the timetable as the meeting proceeds.

You continue: 'I take it that you've studied the minutes of the last meeting.'

(They nod assent.)

'Are there any questions about the minutes?'

(They indicate no questions.)

'Then may I take the minutes as read and sign them on your behalf?'

(They agree. You sign the minutes.)

'Thank you. Now is there any other business so urgent that we must find time for it this morning?'

John: 'Yes, there is one thing. As you know, one of the forklift drivers damned nearly had his head blown off yesterday by a backfire from a Gammal machine. We can't have that happening again and we've got to do something about it – quick!

(You have anticipated this.)

You: 'Yes, I've arranged for a meeting with you, John, Bob and the Safety Officer for 12 noon, today. That should give you time to gather and to sort out the facts. Then

John: 'OK.'
we can give the matter the consideration it deserves. Is
that convenient for you, John?'

You: 'Bob, twelve o'clock convenient for you?'
Bob: 'Yes, fine. The sooner the better.'
You: 'Thank you. The Safety Officer came to see me about it
last night. We'll meet in my office at 12 on that
questions. Anything else that's urgent?'
(Nothing is.)

Any other business

This item has its uses but it can become a mantrap for an
unwary chairman. Any other business is frequently used by
unscrupulous people to slip in matters of self-interest for
which only they have been able to prepare. An example was
brought to me by a distraught chairman who found himself
unable to prevent a resolution being proposed, seconded and
approved by a four-man pressure group within his committee.

The committee consisted of eight members plus chairman.
The chairman was entitled to vote as a member. He also had a
casting vote, if needed. Members were sometimes absent on
other duties. The quorum established by the committee's
constitution required a minimum of five members – plus the
chairman – seven votes in all. At the beginning of the meeting
under consideration six members and the chairman were
present. The four plotters knew that one man had to leave
early. This was the opportunity they had been waiting for.
They used various delaying tactics until his departure, which
left them with a legitimate majority, within the constitution,
of four votes to three. They skipped through the rest of the
agenda and then, under Any Other Business, forced through
exactly what they wanted. Hardly above board but all within
the rules.

The chairman could have prevented this by placing the
question of Any Other Business? early in the proceedings.
And it must be put as a question. The meeting has every right
to say 'No' to an item sprung on them without notice. If the
matter is so desperately urgent that it needs to be dealt with at

once the chairman – with the consent of the members – may rearrange the schedule. It must never be allowed to disrupt the objectives of the meeting as called. As a rule, any extra item should be submitted in writing before the meeting and, if possible, the members should be informed in good time. Remember, Any Other Business? is a request that can be refused.

Let us return to your meeting, Andrew. You had several options in dealing with the business of the backfire incident.

1   You could have allowed it to occupy scarce time at this meeting. But you know that safety at work is no casual matter. The machine has been shut down and the Safety Officer has taken all the required steps. John Betts will fret about the loss of production, Bob Lockyer will make this a union issue and the Safety Officer has a lot of explaining to do – none of which will assist the original purpose of your present meeting. Lucinda has to go to Sheffield but she has already seen you and briefed you on the personnel aspects of the incident.

2   You could have mentioned the matter to all concerned in the coffee room before the meeting. Or handed them a memo – taking their minds off the purpose of the current meeting.

3   You could have evaded the issue and simply told them to sort it out themselves.

4   You could have added the item to this morning's business –probably making a mess of both issues.

In handling it as you did, in just a minute and a half, you gave the backfire meeting the importance it deserves. You made it obvious that you expect them to have all the facts available. You've got the backfire incident out of the way and you are now able with your introductory remarks to make everyone concentrate on the real objectives of this morning's meeting.

You have already established an important control mechanism – time available. Please continue.

Emphasize the objective – define the limits

You: As you all know, the purpose of this meeting is to
          arrive at the date on which we start to build the new
          factory and to progress what we decide. We are not
          here to discuss whether we build or where we build.
          Those matters have been thoroughly examined and we
          need not backtrack. The factory will be located in the
          north east within the area already agreed upon. As was
          set down in your action sheets that went with the
          minutes, every one of you had some investigative
          work to do as a result of our last meeting. We've got
          about an hour and a half. I suggest that we hear what
          each of you has to report, that we filter out anything
          irrelevant to today's purpose then finally pin down an
          acceptable target date that all of us can work to. Will
          that suit everybody?

You take a quick look round. Get a nod or murmured
agreement – being ready to nip in the bud any lengthy
comment that will cloud the purpose as laid down then
continue:

You: Every one of you here is important and we want all
          your views. We have to keep moving. May I suggest
          that each report be presented whole and questions
          arising from it be left until it ends. I've scheduled about
          six minutes for each one. OK?

They agree. Note: Final agreement is your goal. Every 'Yes'
you receive helps you to develop the *yes, yes, yes stream.*
Effective salesmen and effective chairmen know that a series of
negative responses makes a final 'Yes' almost impossible. You
are seeking agreement. Accent the positive. Stimulate 'Yes'
responses whenever you can.

You have planned to begin with Alan Thompson (Finance
Director) and have deliberately placed him at the far end of the
table. He will be using a flip chart and other visual aids. The
equipment is, of course, ready for him.

A poor chairman will deaden a meeting by adopting the
cartwheel method – going round the table from his immediate
left, each member in turn making his contribution in strict
order, until the ball returns to the chair via the fellow on his

immediate right. What happens with such a start? The immediate left member has to use little voice in addressing the chair. He has no eye contact with the rest of the group and needs no projection. A tête-a-tête with the chairman ensues and the rest of the meeting feels unwanted. After this intimate chat, the member left-of-the-immediate-left takes over with similar mumblings. Those on the right hand begin to doze, knowing that it will be an age before their turn – especially as the chairman has reprimanded one of them for butting in out of sequence. When we get to number three, numbers one and two relax, fold their hands and their minds. They will not be needed now for a long, long time and anything they have said is likely to be forgotten, anyway.

Do not let the cartwheel lull your meeting into slumber. Generate a brisk atmosphere. Start with a lively mind at the far end of the table. The speaker will need enough volume in reaching for the chairman to cover and involve the whole meeting.

Begin with an in-common aspect that concerns them all, such as money. Leave more complicated, specialist matters until the general plot has been established, with everybody involved.

You: I thought we'd start with you, Alan. After all we're all interested in money. Is there a money angle that affects the date? Have we got enough? Do we have to borrow some? Is there a taxation factor important to the timing?

Your introductory questioning will give Alan time to gather his wits and to focus the group's attention on him. He will be grateful that you did not jump on him saying: Right! Let's start! Alan!

The action sheet resulting from the last meeting directed him to investigate and to come up with specific answers instead of the estimates he offered previously. This applies to all the members. You have asked them to obtain the facts – and you expect them to deliver their findings in a businesslike manner.

Listen positively

Listen, positively. You will separate fact from opinions and note those facts relevant to the start-up date. You will summarize them later. Also you might need to block sidetracks. Your positive listening will set a good example.

At the end of each presentation you ask only questions for clarification. Do not obviously take over. The last opinion we want is that of the chairman. His views too vigorously expressed could stultify those of members unwilling to cross words with the boss. So, at this stage, questions only asking for clarification – if necessary. Then briefly summarize Alan's main points. When the discussion starts, keep the control by asking specific members for their views. Use someone to the left, someone to the right and so on. They will thus be conditioned to speak through the chair even after you stop leading the questions – as, of course, you will as soon as there is a little cut and thrust in the air.

Alan Thompson's presentation confirms that locating the new plant in the north east, as opposed to building near our present inner-city site, will save several million pounds. Substantial government grants, tax advantages and rates advantages are available in the chosen area: as are docks, sea, railway and airport facilities. A large pool of highly-skilled engineers, craftsmen and general labour seek local employment, etc. The financial case for the proposed site is unanswerable.

Jack Dawson (Production Director) catches your eye, raises his hands and, with a grin, says to you: 'OK, Andrew. I surrender. It's a helluva lot of money.'

Except for a few clarifying questions there is little discussion about money matters at this stage. But Alan has not come to the point about the target date. You need to know this. It is the purpose of the meeting – to obtain a consensus about the date.

You summarize, very briefly, Alan's main facts and the ensuing discussion. (Maggie is carefully noting what you say. Your summaries are probably all that she will use for the minutes.) You then add:

You: 'What about the start-up date for the new building, Alan. This year? Next? When?'

Alan: 'Oh, this year, of course – at least this tax year. Otherwise we lose a whole year's tax advantage. I suggest a couple of months before 4 April next year – say February at the latest.'

You: 'Good. You've made first base – one firm opinion about the date.'

But please note that you had to ask for it: it might have slipped away.

Remind members of the main objective. Keep them on track. Never neglect an opportunity to forge a link in the chain of agreement. One good 'yes' breeds another. Register it. Underline it. Build on it.

Dealing with the shy one

You know from past experience that Graham Todd (Administration and Estates Manager) is terrified of board meetings. His presentation could be a disaster. If you leave him in suspense for too long before bringing him in, he will sit there in a cold sweat biting his fingernails up to the knuckles. So he must be engaged early – not as the opening batsman but, perhaps, at first wicket down: and it must not be a sticky wicket for him. Bring him in on an item or two on which he is an authority and let him score a few comfortable runs. You have planned to ease him into his presentation with this in mind: to get him well into his stride before he realizes that the spotlight is upon him. Even in the preliminary stages of the meeting you have drawn a few responses from him and broken his duck, as it were.

You: 'Right. The money says February. Thank you very much Alan, especially for your summary sheet to remind us of the main figures. As a matter of fact, you have all tabled some damned good handouts. Thank you. It does help: I like your maps and ground plans in particular Graham.'

Lucinda: 'May I ask a question about the plans?'

Since this is a planted question which you have arranged with Lucinda, you say: 'Yes, by all means.'

Lucinda: 'I agree with you, Andrew. These drawings have
             been beautifully done. But I'm not quite clear as to
             where the women's rest room, the cloakrooms and
             the toilet facilities are to be placed in relation to the
             shopfloor: and how much space they get: would
             you please explain, Graham?'
Graham: 'Yes, yes. Of course.'
You: 'I see you've got a large ground plan up there on the
             display board. Perhaps it would be easier for us all if
             you used that.'
             (The Finance Director moves making way for
             Graham.)
You: 'Are you ready, Graham?'
             (Graham nods.)
You: 'Please tell us where the women will rest, hang up
             their coats and powder their noses.'
             (Graham is now on his feet, dealing with a simple
             question. Also, in demonstrating with a visual aid
             he is not bothered about what to do with his hands.
             He answers the question easily.)

   Lucinda says: 'Thank you,' asks perhaps a supplementary
question, which Graham also answers without difficulty.

You: 'All right, Lucinda?'
Lucinda: 'Yes, thank you. Thank you, Graham.'
You: 'As you are there, Graham, perhaps you would like
             to continue. Please do it your way. What news have
             you got for us? For instance have you been able to
             make the right contacts for things like outline
             planning permission?'

   You know that he has: so Graham is able to start with a yes –
a plus for him. Always try to launch a shy one by recognizing
something positive he has achieved. A merited 'well done'
melts the ice and frees the tongue.
   Graham's presentation is not at all bad. He goes into too
much detail unconnected with the target date and you watch
for an opportunity to move him back into what is relevant.
Too crude an interruption will destroy him. In the middle of a
technical fragment about architecture, he dries up. You rescue
him by asking him whether you have his facts clear, so far.

You summarize. Meanwhile, Graham recovers. You lead him on to his next stage with a simple question arising from your summary.

Interim summaries

Interim summaries provide you with a useful control device. You can use an interim summary:

1   To cover a hiatus, as above with Graham: to help and to stimulate a waverer.
2   To simplify too complicated an offering.
3   To separate the irrelevant from the relevant and to emphasize the latter.
4   To change the pace and direction of the discussion.
5   To stop the flow of the tub-thumper, the pretentious, the irrelevant or even the offensive.
6   To bring the ball back into your own court when the meeting becomes either too slack or too heated. You talk calmly and long enough to let the shouting die: then relocate the focus to a more useful member (bland or vigorous, as required). You might switch to an oblique, even different aspect – a fresh angle on the subject as well as a fresh speaker. At the end of your summary, the ball is under your control to distribute as you wish.
7   To serve as an opportunity to clinch what they have already agreed on. To show that they are making progress.
8   To isolate points not yet agreed and to begin discussing them in a climate of 'We are agreed on . . . Now. . . !'

Keep an eye on the time. At present, you are within schedule.

Dealing with the quarrelsome

The next presentation is likely to be contentious and could descend into a Bob Lockyer (Labour Relations) versus John Betts (Works Manager) brawl. Sacred cows are at risk from both of them. Summon up your strengths, your controls. Display them and remind the members that they apply to everyone. At the end of Graham's presentation and the ensuing discussions, you prepare the ground for Bob Lockyer's contribution – in your own way, of course, on these lines:

You: 'Thank you, Graham. Your professional opinion is that all such matters as planning permission, tenders, contracts, etc., can be sorted out by November. That fits in nicely with Alan's February date. Well done. So far, so good. We'd like to hear from you now, Bob.'
(As Bob moves into position.)

You: 'We're well up to time, but could I remind you all that we must finish by 1045 and we must keep to things relevant to a decision on the target date. OK? Ready Bob?'

As you expected, Bob has discussed the manning of the new plant with the TUC at Headquarters and has already established a union network at local levels. He continues:

Bob: 'Although people will be mighty glad to get the jobs, none of you must run away with the idea that you're going to get them on the cheap, like Mr Thompson seems to be suggesting. A fair day's work is worth a fair day's pay at rates decided by the unions.'
(John Betts interrupts. He snaps:)

John: 'No! Oh, no! Not decided by the unions. Negotiated with us and the unions. Negotiated, mate, negotiated.'
(Bob is about to retaliate, when you stop him with a gently raised hand.)

You: 'Just a minute, Bob. I think we'd better let Bob finish, John. We want your views later. So save it.'
(You continue and take the focus away from the combatants. Turning to Lucinda:)

You: 'Matters such as recruitment, wages and conditions are matters for you, Bob, and Miss Carson to discuss at the appropriate time. That is so, isn't it, Lucinda?'

Lucinda: 'Yes, of course: but certainly not here and now.'

You:	'Thank you. Now, Bob, have you anything to add that affects the target date?'
Bob:	'No, not really. I'm ready now. The sooner the better.'

Nevertheless, he goes on. Bob is a cunning negotiator and he senses an opportunity to put Betts in the wrong. To exhibit John Betts as a consistently loud-mouthed windbag could be useful on some future occasion. Bob knows that he, himself, must radiate innocence while offering a bait that will stab a raw wound and bring Mr Betts to the boil. He concludes his remarks with:

Bob:	'So the men and women who do the work will be properly organized, and treated with respect – unless, of course, we want the sort of industrial action we got a couple of years ago. And we all know how that started. Ham-fisted management. We were all to blame for that one, including me.'
John:	'You speak for yourself – you and your bloody union. Don't you start threatening us with your strikes even before the factory's built.'
Bob:	'Well, I was only . . .'
John:	'No, no. You're not going to shut me up. I know what you're hinting at. You're getting at me. So I sacked a couple of troublemakers and put their noses out of joint.'
Bob:	(Sweetly reasonable) 'Seventeen hundred workers had their noses put out of joint and the six weeks without any production cost the firm three million quid.'

Of course, Betts explodes into a noisy self-defence. Let us leave him for a while.

Andrew, you have various means at your disposal to put a stop to this vulgar skirmish. Preferably you should nip it in the bud immediately.

1 You could use the fact that what they are squabbling about is irrelevant to the target date.
2 You could use the time contol.
3 You could sum up Bob's presentation and pass on to the next.

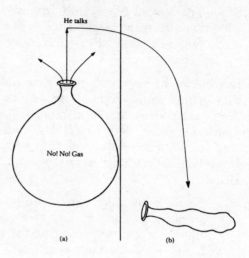

He talks

No! No! Gas

(a)   (b)

Figure 2

4   You could order both of them to shut up at once, leaving
    Bob with a cheap victory and John Betts a raging volcano –
    clamped down, but still raging underneath. If left in this
    state, John would take back to his office a seething rancour
    that will permeate the entire department for weeks.

May we digress for a moment in order to consider another
method of dealing with the loud and the quarrelsome?

What are the facts of the Betts and Lockyer issue? Some time
back, when you and Tony Sharp were on a selling mission in
the United States, John Betts had strongly resented the
intrusion of two workhands into his office with what he called
'demands'. The pair represented a small clique of politically-
motivated rogues, and their calculated purpose was to make
Betts overreact. They succeeded. A fracas ensued, culminat-
ing in Betts sacking both of them on the spot: also providing
them with a burning cause – an 'injustice' with which to
inflame the shopfloor. The incident was deliberately whipped
up into a bitter strike lasting several weeks. Subsequently,
Lucinda Carson was brought in to strengthen the personnel
side. But Betts has never been allowed to forget. And, when
goaded, he roars.

Why do some men and women erupt at the slightest
provocation? The short answer is that they are not accustomed

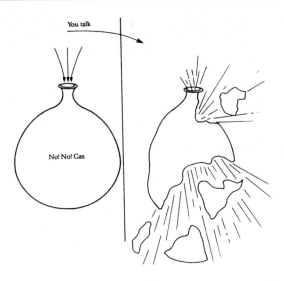

Figure 3

to being heeded. So they shout to arrogate attention. So people heed them even less. The last reaction Loudmouth expects is that somebody will actually listen to what he has to say. Let us surprise him. Let us listen. Man learns more by listening than by talking. That is why the good God gave us two eyes, two ears and only one mouth. Somewhere, smothered in Loudmouth's guff and bugaboo, there might possibly be a valuable point. We won't be able to recognize it if we try to outblast him. Please look at the balloon in Figure 2.

At (a) the balloon is stretched full of a gas called 'No! No!'. It could perhaps, present an objection to your sales pitch. Your customer is protesting, saying 'No! No!'. If you encourage him to talk, thus releasing the gas, the balloon will shrivel into (b). In the meantime, you listen and come to understand his objection. Only then can you deal with it sensibly.

If, on the other hand, you try to out-talk your customer – forcing in yet more gas – there will shortly be an explosion as the balloon bursts in your face (Figure 3).

As an old Welsh railwayman once remarked: 'Collision – there you are. Explosion – where the bloody hell are you?'

Listen. Let your customer deflate his own balloon.

To treat his noisy objection with equally loud contempt simply confirms his opinion that whatever he says you will not even consider it. To win a heated argument often means to lose an ally and a friend. In particular, you never win an argument with a customer. The mouth is the enemy of the sale.

We can apply the same principle to a blusterer at meetings. If you want Loudmouth to share your views, do not try to bash them into his skull with a pickaxe. Agreement, like the quality of mercy, is not strained.

'It is a matter of communications' is a phrase often repeated but not always fully understood. Communication is more than talking or writing. What measures the effectiveness of a communication is the reaction it stimulates. Unless the recipient responds in the way you wish, you have not communicated: you have merely talked – a one-way process. Communication works two ways: what you send out and what comes back. And it is what comes back that tells the score. To communicate means to share (Latin v. communicare from which stem all sorts of words implying something shared, e.g. commune, community, communism, commonwealth, communion [we share in a sacrament] communication, common and, by extension, in common.) You want the other fellow to share your views, to think and to act in common with your wishes.

You seek consensus at your meetings, agreement. Part of your duty as a chairman is to create an environment that enables agreement to flourish.

You seek agreement, not surrender. It is as well at this stage to establish the distinction between these words. Imagine that you have a chap on the floor. You have your foot on his neck and a loaded gun in your hand. Six of your friends, big, burly prop-forward types, all carrying guns, also menace this unfortunate wretch. You stamp on his face, cock your gun and snarl, 'Do you agree?' What does he say? He says 'Yes'. Your friends go home. You put your gun away and turn your back on the wretch only to find that there is a knife in it – in your back, I mean. Because what you got was not agreement, it was surrender. Failure to understand the difference between these two words causes most of our industrial troubles. Surrender rarely settles anything for long. Agreement works.

Agreement is impossible while the parties are at war, actually fighting. Agreement is unlikely to be achieved during

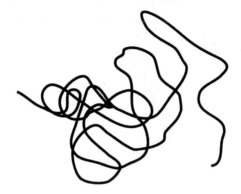

Figure 4

a quarrel, even during a heated argument. Agreement cannot begin until we discuss our differences. A skilled chairman brings the dispute to a discussion of a relevant question as soon as possible – before too many offensive remarks have soured the participants, before too many fixed attitudes have been developed. Few angry men will retract, recant, withdraw. Even fewer will apologize and agree that they were wrong. So get in quickly. Minimize the heat and get to a question – for discussion.

Let the tangled wire in Figure 4 represent Loudmouth in full spate; distorted, illogical, offensive. One cannot discuss such chaos. You must bring the meeting to a question as soon as possible by straightening and reshaping the wire as in Figure 5.

First step: Isolate Loudmouth by instructing the meeting to give him their attention for, say, two uninterrupted minutes. The members will usually accept this as reasonable.

Second step: Give Loudmouth his head. Let him expose himself.

Third step: *Listen.* Give him your full attention and interest. Resist the temptation to seem bored or impatient. Look him straight in the eye and listen, positively. Remember, he is not used to being heard unchallenged. If he has something pertinent to say, you will be able to spot it. If not, alone and naked to the full glare of the spotlight and with many pairs of eyes on him, he will realize that he is talking rubbish and probably come to a full stop. It goes like this:

Figure 5

Loudmouth: 'Blah! Blah! Blah! Blah! Myer! Myer! Myer! Myer! Scrur! Scrur! Scrur! Scrur!'

– and so on until he makes an outlandish statement. Even he discerns that he has gone over the top. He hesitates. There follows an eerie silence with everybody eagerly waiting.

Loudmouth: 'Oh, well – that's what I think, anyway (or some such lame ending).'

My management training colleagues and many of my business friends have worked this technique during seminars and at about a hundred real business meetings. The observed average time for a Loudmouth to bring himself to a grinding halt is a remarkable forty-eight seconds.

Add this ploy to your control equipment but watch out for the professional gab merchant who can talk and talk for hours and say nothing – a politician, for instance, who answers, with dollops of party cant, any question but the one he has just been asked. Do not offer such a smoothie your platform. If he takes it anyway, vary your technique. Again, and importantly, listen. Discourage interrupters. Listen. At some juncture he will leave you an opening to use the twisted wire device. You want to discuss a question not to listen to a diatribe. You want him to agree, to say 'yes'. Bring in the Yes, Yes, Yes stream. Every 'yes' you gain strengthens your control. You stop him politely by asking him to clarify something – not because he is being obscure (Heaven forbid!) but because you (silly duffer) have failed to grasp his meaning. You say:

You:	'That's very interesting, very interesting indeed, but I'm not quite certain about your reference to American salary structures (Don't stop yet. Get a question in, requiring the answer 'yes'.) It's apparently different from ours. Is that so?'
Loudmouth:	Yes it is. (One 'Yes'.) (Now the twisted wire and the yes, yes, yes stream development.)
You:	'Please correct me if I'm wrong' (by now you have dammed the flow of claptrap) 'Is the question you are asking: Should we adopt a similar system in this country?'
Loudmouth:	'That's right. Yes. (Another yes.)
You:	'And you think it might be useful if we discussed your question?'
Loudmouth:	'Yes.' (What else can he do but agree. Another yes.)

You now have a question to discuss, not a harangue to suffer. If the subject is relevant to the objective of your meeting you can put the question. If it is not relevant, you thank Loudmouth and give him a ladder to climb down.

You:	'Thank you very much. It's an important question but I think you will agree that it's not really relevant to our present purpose. Nevertheless it is something we ought to look at. Would you like to put it on the agenda for another meeting? It could be very useful and we could give your idea more time.'
Loudmouth:	'Thank you. Yes.' (He hasn't disagreed with you once.)

But do not loiter. Any hesitation on your part now will be interpreted by Loudmouth as an invitation to reopen the floodgates. Keep talking, calmly. Use a brief summary to bring the meeting back into line. You have chosen Lucinda to pick up the thread. She will be factual, pleasant and authoritative, exactly what is needed to sink Loudmouth for the rest of the meeting and to restore progress.

Among other things, Lucinda has been head-hunting and already she has a shortlist of potential managers for the new plant. She suggests that we engage the top four managers now, so that they can work at our present plant to gain experience of the company, the products and key customers. They must also acquire sufficient knowhow and teamwork to enable them to cooperate with her in selection and recruitment when the new factory is ready. Lucinda does not mention this but she, too, has developed a network at high level; not only with employers' organizations and the local authorities, but also with her friends in the unions – a much more powerful and better balanced network than Bob Lockyer's. She agrees to a target date round about December, which harmonizes with the others already suggested.

Tony Sharp enthuses about glowing sales prospects – backed up by facts. His target date is today – but he will settle for December.

Albert Fox, who has been working closely with Tony and John Betts about deliveries of finished goods and raw materials, can organize transport within budget and by the year's end. So far, so good.

Now, the bombshell.

Jack Dawson (Production Director) has been rather subdued. He now presents us with a problem that might upset all the dates so far proposed. We need sixteen Gammal machines for the new plant. The manufacturers have only two machines readily available, and seven in progress. Dawson has placed an order for these, subject to our confirmation within one month. The normal lead time for making the remaining seven machines would be eighteen months: but they can be expedited for a late December delivery if we pay an extortionate premium for extra shift working, for overtime and for monopolizing their worklines, thus inhibiting sales to other customers.

This extra cost will completely wreck our financial planning. We simply cannot afford it.

The discussion becomes animated. Tony Sharp will brook no delay. His team can double sales within two years; but, at the latest, our product must be coming off the lines by April or May next year. We are already keeping customers waiting.

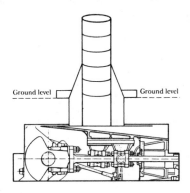

Figure 6

Without an abundance of additional production, we will not only fail to conquer new markets, but we will also be unable to satisfy the customers we already have. 'Let us find the money,' he declares, 'or else!'

Lucinda suggests that we proceed with the building, using nine machines, and install the others later.

Dawson explains that that would mean knocking down most of the building we have just erected.

Lucinda: 'But why?'

Jack: 'Well, to start with, these machines are forty-five feet high and fifty feet at the base.'

Lucinda: 'Oh, surely not. I've seen. . . .'

Jack: 'You've only seen what's at ground level.'
(He goes to a flip chart and draws a rough sketch – Figure 6.)
(He emphasizes the colossal size and weight and continues.)

Jack: 'You try getting that lot through a brick wall. We've got to excavate, lay the foundations, put in all the wiring; and the pipework, et cetera, et cetera and et cetera, and a helluva lot more et ceteras. The machines have to go in first and the factory shell built round them.'

Lucinda: 'I see.'

Tony: 'Well, that's your headache, Jack. All I want is something to sell and my customers satisfied because we deliver on time. So let's find the money and get cracking.'

The time is 10.34.

Andrew, you realize that the money problem cannot be dealt with by this group. Your full board must discuss a solution in private. You explain this. But you do not want to lose momentum by leaving the target date dangling in space and the departments without direction. A lame, negative ending will not do. You must ensure that the participants go away from this meeting – indeed from all your meetings – feeling that they have done a good job and have contributed to a success. Accentuate the positive. You sum up and gain their consent that January seems to be the most suitable date to start the new building. We met to establish a target date. Now we have a target date to work to. 'Well done. Thank you.'

As is customary at your meetings, each member agrees on his or her post-meeting actions. The action sheets will form an integral part of the minutes. You never form sub-committees. You name one person only. If he or she wishes to engage others to share the load that's up to the individual. Numbers may help in carrying a load: but numbers dilute responsibility and the greater the number the easier it becomes to dodge the onus.

You thank them, announce the date for their next meeting and send them on their way rejoicing (or, at least, feeling pretty good).

Andrew, you now face a difficult task, for money is a demanding taskmaster. Several tricky meetings loom.

There is an exercise for you below, but, before we go into it, please review your handling of the target-date meeting by responding fully to these questions:

Beforehand

1   Did you define and refine:
   (a)   the precise purpose of the meeting?
   (b)   the subject under discussion and the scope – the limits within which you must keep the discussion in order to forestall irrelevancies and to achieve your objective?

2   Did you:
   (a)   check that you have invited all and only the right people to get the business done?
   (b)   pause for a while to appreciate their value as specialists: also did you ensure that you possess sufficient knowledge of their specialities – at least to the level of an intelligent layman? If not, did you fill in the gaps?
   (c)   anticipate any personal difficulties the participants might have – or cause?
3   Did you:
   (a)   check with your Number One (Maggie) that she has completed her side of the arrangements?
   (b)   discuss your brief with her?
   (c)   reread the documentation? (Skim through it, anyway.)
4   Did you:
   (a)   work out a time schedule?
   (b)   prepare opening remarks that will enable you to lay down the track and to establish controls?

At the meeting

Did you:
1   start on time?
2   set a good example by being agreeable, businesslike – and brief?
3   clarify the objectives, the scope of the meeting?
4   remind everyone that they are *all* important and that we need their help in this matter?
5   establish and obtain their tacit agreement to the modus operandi – the 'rules', time limits, your controls, etc?
6   begin with a brisk contributor at the far end of the table?
7   listen and, by keeping a roving eye on them, ensure that everyone else listened?

Along the track

Did you:

1 keep the members to the point?
2 evaluate ideas constructively?
3 help to clarify anything obscure?
4 make full use of summaries?
5 deal fairly and effectively with both the mild and the wild?
6 obtain a progressive result from each presentation?
7 obtain a satisfactory discussion, a final decision and businesslike action from the whole meeting?

Did your members depart knowing that they had done useful work?

You will find a full chairmanship checklist in Appendix 2, page 112.

Exercise

1 *For the chairman*

1 List the several meetings that might arise subsequent to your next board meeting – the one about the money problem.
2 Take any one of them, for instance with the machine makers. Prepare to negotiate a more responsible price. What steps do you take in advance of the meeting to strengthen your hand. Never underestimate the opposition or yourself. Know the facts. Know the margins:
   • What are your plus points?
   • Where are you vulnerable?
   • What are the plus points for the opposition?
   • Where are they vulnerable?
3 Quick-read this chapter once more.
4 Prepare to chair the meeting. How can you win?
   Note: This case study is based on a real incident. I suggest that you first work on it solo – and thoroughly. If you can then combine with, say, a management training group within your own organization, you will find the exercise most valuable.

You have a choice of meetings, e.g. with your bankers, your stockbrokers, your shareholders, government bodies, building contractors and others.

For the Number One

1 Write up the minutes of the target date meeting, bearing in mind that several board members who were elsewhere need to know.
2 Outline what is required from you in advance of the next meeting – paperwork etc.

8   A member of the meeting

Thirty two thousand, nine hundred and eighty three people attended the local cup-tie. George was one of them. Press, radio and television reporters went into raptures about the player who scored the winning goal. The directors, the manager, the team, the team coach, the physio – even the programme sellers and the tea ladies exulted. They had achieved something. Who would have noticed if George had been elsewhere? Only the man counting the gate money: but he cares little because he, too, had taken an active part in the triumph. At this meeting George was merely present, signifying nothing but a number.

Do you have a George at your business meetings? and – perish the thought! – are you just a George? Of course you are not. You never attend a meeting merely to warm a seat.

Few people think seriously about meetings even when meetings form their principal daily activity. As a director, a manager or an aspiring manager you will be interested in facts. A survey of over 5000 men and women such as yourself revealed the following data:

- On average, they had each received about fourteen years of formal education.
- Approximately one-third of them gained degrees, diplomas or other paper qualifications.
- Only one in twenty-three felt that their subsequent achievements in life matched their abilities, qualifications or early ambitions.
- Fewer than one in twenty had been taught such skills as effective speaking and handling meetings.

Their general experience was that they had been thrown in at the deep end and forced to learn by their mistakes. A do-it-yourself brain surgeon could stand on a heap of shattered skulls and boast that he had now got the hang of it.

If, privately, you do not feel fully equipped as a meeting man, now is the time to start putting the matter right.

Many business meetings produce nothing but frustration and expense. The average executive spends a third of his working life talking at interviews, conferences and committees (to say nothing of the cost, the time and the hassle involved in getting there and back). How much of this talk is productive? How many businessmen and women are either confident or competent when making a presentation. All forms of communication are a struggle for other people's attention – and the competition is fierce.

When you were recruited, at your job interview, you were assessed by your seniors and considered the right man to fill their needs. They knew little about you and, as always on such occasions, were obliged to trust their judgement of you – and to hope. At every subsequent meeting, in the light of greater knowledge, they cumulatively adjust their evaluation of your worth for better or for worse. Meetings lay bare a man's true qualities. They provide a ladder to help him to climb to the top: or they can become grim test-beds where he is judged and found wanting.

Your directors judge you at meetings. Your peers judge you at meetings. Your subordinates judge you at meetings. Your customers judge you at meetings. Only a George doodles through life as an onlooker. You will wish to take an active part and to influence the outcome of every meeting. To be there is not enough.

Lady Luck smiles on those ready to receive her bounty. She laughs outright at those who muff their chances because they are unready to capitalize on them.

Before the meeting

Being an effective member of a meeting demands as much preparation as being in the chair; *sometimes more.*

As a member of a meeting your main task is to help the chairman to complete the business in hand. But suppose you disagree with the proposals on his agenda? Then your aim will be to help the chairman to complete the business in hand more effectively than he could have done without you; to bring facts to bear; to persuade him and the others that your way is better for them; to make them glad that you were invited. This means, in effect, that you need to have a firmer grasp of the situation than anyone else. Also you need to disagree without being disagreeable. The trick is to disagree with the opinion, not the person holding it. Above all you must not cause the chairman to lose face. He can be your staunchest ally. If he is less than competent, you can be his rescuer and his friend. It follows that you must understand the chairman's intentions, his problems, his needs and the conditions under which his meeting will operate. What levels of formality will he expect? What are the procedures within which the meeting will work, the rules, as it were. In the preceding chapter, the chairman was recommended to answer several preliminary questions. You must also consider them and select those pertinent to yourself as a member. For instance, if the documentation you receive is not clear, obtain clarification. Ask his Number One. At least prepare yourself by considering:

1   Am I completely clear about the purpose of the meeting?
2   Am I positive about what my contribution should be?
3   What information do I need from others?
4   What information are others likely to need from me?
5   Have I the authority to agree to decisions reached?
6   Do I know who is likely to support me, and who is not?
7   What points must I stick to?
8   Where can I compromise?
9   What action do I want from the meeting?
10   Am I thoroughly prepared to make a first-class contribution – and to win?

Some of these questions will demand that you get to work. Preparation pays dividends. Surprisingly, you will often find that you are the only member with the advantage of forethought.

At the start

You are punctual, of course. You are genial, of course. You

are attentive to the chairman's opening remarks. If the chairman sets out a workmanlike framework for the meeting, give him your, preferably tacit, assent. If he does not, ask well-mannered questions to clarify the situation. Avoid any suggestion that you are usurping his authority. Do not tell him that he is wrong. Ask for his guidance. Recognize the chair. Respect the chairman. But, if he is a lame duck, help him to lay down a firm framework at the start. You might even help to establish some of his control points, such as time, tactfully, of course – by asking for his guidance, his ruling. Avoid any suggestion of sycophancy. You are one of his team. He will be grateful for the opportunity you give him to amend his briefing should he need to do so. He will be better prepared at subsequent meetings. Many a boss has been educated by his subordinates without being aware of the fact.

On the way

A marathon runner with 26 miles and 385 yards to go makes no attempt to cover the first mile in four minutes flat. He would soon run out of puff if he did. The London to Edinburgh Express does not speed away from the terminus at a hundred miles an hour. Like a soldier picking his way through a minefield, the driver carefully observes and negotiates the myriad inner-city hazards, using full power only when conditions become appropriate. Many a Grand National hopeful has been bought down in the stampede to be in the lead at the first fence. A poker player conceals his hand until the right moment. There is a right moment for you to be prominent at a meeting: it is rarely good tactics to blow your trumpet early in the proceedings.

If necessary – but only if it has been necessary – you have already ensured, by discreetly asking for his guidance, that the chairman has declared a workmanlike structure for the meeting. Now is the time for you to imagine that you are a small boy who has been ordered by his Victorian father 'to speak only when you are spoken to'. Now is the time for you to look and listen; to sense the atmosphere; to weigh up the other members; to assess their values and intentions. An open mouth is not the channel through which the mind digests food for thought. One does not ask for the opinion of a man who has already foisted it upon the meeting. An opinion requested is likely to be listened to. During the opening exchanges, a few minutes of golden silence can be most instructive and of immense tactical value.

Keep this notion in mind throughout the meeting. The art of timing distinguishes great performers from the mediocre. Choose your moment to make your contribution. Never join in the hurly-burly when arguments run hot. Let the blusterers show their hands. Let them waste their substance. Listen. Separate facts from assertions. When the combatants have talked themselves into such a nasty tangle that neither side can give way, your objective solution could loosen the knots and save all their faces. Use your ammunition sparingly. One bullet is enough when all the others have been spent.

If the chairman knows his job, just work with him. If not, work for him. For instance, if the meeting gets out of hand, ask politely whether you have got the facts clear so far. 'I may be wrong, Mr Chairman, but as I see it the facts are . . .' (interim summing up) and ask for his ruling.

You can devise ways of bringing all the chairman's controls into play. But do not try to score points off him. Give him the final yes or no as to what is and what is not in order. If you see rocks ahead, make the Captain aware of the fact, but let him decide whether or not to alter course. Your job as a member is to help the chairman to achieve the objectives of the meeting, not to take over (at least not to be caught doing so).

An interlude

Passing the buck or six characters in search of a scapegoat

Chambers Twentieth Century Dictionary defines a scapegoat as:

> A goat on which, once a year, the Jewish high priest laid symbolically the sins of the people, and which was then allowed to escape into the wilderness. (Lev. XVI): any animal used in like manner: one who is made to bear the misdeeds of another.

The scene is a beautifully appointed boardroom. Elegant

pictures adorn the walls, prominent among them an oil painting of the company's Edwardian founder, who looks down upon the assembled directors with something approaching disdain. A well-stocked bar stands conspicuously against a wall. As the curtain rises we see a red-faced, almost tearful engineer leaving the room. Malcolm, one of the directors, violently closes the door with his foot.

Malcolm: 'God's truth! I need a drink.'
Richard: 'Don't we all?'
(The meeting adjourns to the bar)
Malcolm: (Outside a large Scotch in one gulp) 'What a damn waste of time.'
Kevin: 'I've come all the way from Dublin to hear that rubbish.'
Thomas: 'I still have no idea what he was talking about.'
Malcolm: 'I don't think he had, either.'
Kevin: 'Why did we let him in at all?'
Thomas: 'Why do we let any of them in? There was the waffler we had in last month; the crawler the month before, and before that the personnel bloke snivelling about pregnant women on the shopfloor – and every one of them pleading for money.'
Kevin: 'They seem to think we're made of the stuff. We're not a charity. We're in business.'
Mark: 'We won't be that much longer by the look of things. You called this meeting, Richard. What was it all supposed to be about?'
Richard: 'You know perfectly well. I sent you a memo.'
Mark: 'I remember. It said: "to discuss a suggestion for an improvement on the production line making a considerable saving and extra profitability notwithstanding a modicum of downturn in the course of the implementation of the scheme and the consequent reinstallation of the relevant machinery during the period." How's that for a dollop of gobbledegook?'
Richard: 'It seems clear enough to me.'
Mark: 'Did you send us any information for us to think about – a brief outline of the case, drawings, plans, costs, etc?'

Richard:	'The fellow didn't give me any more details than I set out in the memo.'
Mark:	'Did you ask him for more?'
Richard:	'No. I can't waste time running after everybody making a presentation.'
Mark:	'So instead of just you we all wasted our time. Pity.'
Richard:	'Look here! Are you blaming me for that blithering idiot's performance?'
Mark:	'Yes, I am. And I'll share the blame with you. We all ought to.'
Richard:	'I don't see what more we can do than to hire qualified people and let them get on with the job. That fellow is a graduate and should be able to express himself. He should learn the hard way, like I had to.'
Mark:	'Well, since you raise the point, you're not exactly in the Queen's Counsel class when it comes to advocacy. We lost the Anderson contract because you made a lousy presentation to their board. Bill Anderson told me so himself. And that's not the only one. Kevin, what about the flop at Galloways?'
Richard:	'Before you get too high and mighty, what about your sales force? They're not exactly bringing in the orders in bundles. Whose fault's that?'
Mark:	'I'm well aware of the dismal sales figures. Most of my pay is based on commission – you don't have to tell me.'
Richard:	'Well then, stop being a pot calling the kettle black.'
Mark:	'Do you know how much money we've spent on sales training in the last three years?'
Richard:	'As a matter . . .'
Mark:	'Don't bother. The answer is not a penny.'
Richard:	'We can't afford . . .'
Arnold:	'Hold on a minute. Let me fill your glass up, Ric. Mark? Beer, wasn't it, same as mine? Top up? Help yourself to another one, Kevin. In fact, we all need another one. Cheers!'
Several:	'Cheers!'

Arnold:	(quietly) 'Before we get into too much of a lather, let's agree on something. We can't go on as we are, can we? Agreed?'
Several:	'Yes. Agreed. Too true, etc.'
Arnold:	'Then where do we start to put things right? I suggest here in the boardroom. Before we criticize other people's pimples let us examine our own boils. Does anybody out there in the offices and the workshops and the labs know what we expect of them when they come in here to put forward a proposal? Even more to the point – do we ourselves know what we require from them?'
Several:	'Well, it's obvious . . .'
	'What's the . . .'
	'Any damned fool knows . . .'
	'We want them to talk business . . .'
Arnold:	'You're all full of ideas. Look. We've got about twenty minutes before we go into lunch. Let's all sit down separately for five minutes and jot down what we think we need from a presenter. OK? Five minutes silence, no chat, think awhile and scribble away. Let's start.'
	(They do so. In the balm of silence, tempers cool and the clock is ignored. At the end of fifteen minutes, they are still scribbling away – ideas in abundance. Arnold stops them.)
Arnold:	'Shall I tell you what's in my mind?'
Several:	'Yes.'
	'Yes.'
	'Yes.'
	'Yes, what's in your mind, Arnold?'
Arnold:	'It's a bit like finding out what the customer wants instead of trying to sell him what we've got. Do you think it might be more productive if, instead of issuing an instruction to presenters, we put to them what we, their customers as it were, want and encouraged them to meet our needs?'
Malcolm:	'It sounds arse-uppards to me. Why not a straight-forward order – do this and do that?'
Arnold:	'Because I think Mark is right. We're all to blame and we've got to lead by example and the best

	starting point is for us to clear our own minds, to be sure – as the customer – what we want from our suppliers, the presenters.'
Mark:	'So what you propose is that we create a statement of the board's needs from a presenter, a sort of specification?'
Arnold:	'That's it. We've already got a couple of hundred ideas between us. Suppose we have a quick meeting to sort out what's important and to shape an outline. It should only take about an hour. I'll volunteer to write it up.'
Mark:	'Sounds good to me. When?'
Arnold:	'Today if possible, as we're all here. It's urgent.'
Richard:	'Can't do today. Got Martinson for lunch. Won't get rid of him before five.'
Arnold:	'What about six thirty to seven thirty?'
Kevin:	'That's no good for me. My flight goes at 1750.'
Arnold:	'Can't you change it and go tomorrow?'
Kevin:	'Molly's expecting me.'
Arnold:	'Ring her up. She'll understand.'
Kevin:	'No, sorry.'
Thomas:	'You can count me out, too. We've got seats for *Miss Saigon*. Not going to throw them away.'

One by one, they found an excuse to dodge the issue. No action today. No action tomorrow or next week. No action at all. The matter was quietly dropped as too much trouble. It was much more comforting to lay the blame on those stupid creatures called *them*.

At a board meeting several months later, a young man called Jonathan all but wrecked his career prospects by making an appalling presentation. The board heard him through to the end because they sensed that, somewhere buried in his inept blather, he might have a great idea. They thanked him, told him they'd 'let him know' and hustled him out of the room. The managing director turned to one of his colleagues and said: (I've cleaned up the language) 'Arnold, that clot might have something there. Would you please have a look at it and come back to us at the next board meeting with the facts?'

From that moment, Arnold took possession of Jonathan's brain-child. He also took credit for the substantial profits accruing from the brain-child's subsequent development. Jonathan was marked down as useless. Dismissal was in the air.

There is a happy ending to this sad little tale. Perhaps I had better explain to you why I was at this meeting. At Arnold's insistence the company had called upon the management training organization to which I belong to assess their training needs and to make recommendations. The board members were somewhat surprised and not a little huffy when my team insisted on starting our observations at the top. The board's attitude provided an immediate warning signal. When top brass considers training as something for only the lower orders, it often indicates a hardening of their commercial arteries. No wonder this company was in decline.

The boardroom is the powerhouse from which the whole organization draws strength for good or ill. If the leadership lacks commercial health their sickness filters through all the way down to the office boy. Every one of these directors went regularly to their medicos for a physical check-up. That their management skills might also need care and maintenance had not occurred to them. Fortunately they soon saw the light, which they had been hiding under a bushel: for they were first-rate men despite being afflicted by a coating of rust and incipient decay. On completion of our survey, they agreed to the proposed training programme. In particular, they accepted that we should begin at the top, with themselves.

Early workshops with the board focused on presentations: how to eliminate what became known as the Jonathan syndrome. Alas, Jonathan was by no means unique. The company had done nothing in the way of developing communications skills within the organization. Jonathans abounded among the older managers. Young high-flyers had been grounded, or had departed. Technicians and scientists, cosily holed-up within their own specialities, were reluctant to bring the results of their work to the board. Thus, many a profitable concept went begging. Even the sales force laboured without know-how, flair – or sufficient orders. At least half of the board members, terrified at the prospect of speaking, were operating at less than their potential to present themselves and their company to full effect. The balance sheet reflected this deplorable state of affairs. To echo Mark

Anthony: If ye have shares to shed, prepare to shed them now. But wait. Hold on. There is hope.

Every business meeting should have a clear-cut objective. A training session is no exception. From every business meeting profitable action should ensue. A training session is no exception.

We decided to tackle their problems with presentations in two stages:

1   To improve their speaking ability for any occasion – basic techniques.
2   To concentrate on the special requirements for a successful business presentation.

*   *   *

You have been patient during this temporary diversion – looking at other people's troubles. Does this sort of thing happen within your own sphere of activity? Do you need to make presentations as part of your job: or to consider presentations made to you? Are you a first-class speaker? What follows is, of course, for you.

9 Effective speaking

Successful managers at any level are good communicators, but this skill doesn't come giftwrapped to anybody. You have the talent but this talent has to be thought about, worked on and developed. Techniques are simply tricks of the trade that make a job easier. In a letter to me (the late) Lord Mancroft remarked: 'Some people think that speaking, like sex, ought to come to us all naturally. Maybe it should: but in both cases it's just as well to learn a few tricks.' As a professional communicator, the time you invest on mastering basic speaking techniques will pay dividends.

Effective speaking stimulates the desired reaction. There is no other criterion. How to stimulate the required reaction: that's what we shall be looking at.

The main factor in *successful speaking* is to concentrate on the audience, both in your preparation and your delivery. *It's your fault* if you don't speak effectively. May I ask you to consider the following proposition:

> That the only obstacle preventing you from speaking effectively is your own vanity, your conceit, your self-centred worry about yourself.

Please do not reject – or even accept – this proposition without giving it thought. Pause for a moment, ask yourself, 'Is this chap talking nonsense or can it be that vanity causes my speaking trouble?' Think about it for five minutes – please – honestly. Where is your focus, on them or on yourself?

Let us look at three aspects of speaking:

1 Audiences: your attitude to them and their attitude to you.
2 Preparation.
3 Delivering the goods.

An audience is a group of agreeable people much like

yourself. They have their problems – family problems, social problems, tax problems, health problems – just like you. They come to hear you speak and they come with an immense amount of goodwill. They want you to succeed. What they succeed in getting out of your talk is the measure of your success.

Definition: *a successful speaker is one who gives his audience a success.*

Your job as a speaker is to give the audience a fair exchange for the time and attention they give to you – not to worry about yourself. So get your focus firmly on your audience. Do not ask 'How am I going to do?' Ask yourself, instead, 'How are they going to do?' With very few exceptions there is no such thing as an audience you need to fear. Just get your focus right and build your success on their goodwill.

Now let's turn the penny over. An audience is not in the least bit interested in you or your subject until what you have to say has something to do with them. Obviously, you must link what you have to say to your audience and their interests. So long as you know your subject, effective speaking stems almost entirely from a study and consideration of other people. Never worry about speaking – work at it. Get yourself ready to do the job properly.

Stage one – preparation

To start with, gather lots of material – enough for ten times the length of the talk you intend to give. Write down (at great speed so that ideas flood on to the paper) every aspect of your subject that enters your head.

Persevere until you have facts, opinions, examples, direct thoughts, oblique and tangential thoughts, points central to your topic and points on the edges of it. Get everything down in notes, headings or any other rapid form that will enable you to recall the ideas when you start the next stage in your preparation – the planning stage.

Don't linger with thinking ideas through at this preliminary stage – get the notes down fast – hundreds of them. Ignore nothing, however trivial, ponder on nothing, however important. Just set the notions down. If you have three weeks to prepare, the jottings stage should fully occupy one of them. If you have an hour, use twenty minutes pouring the ideas on to paper. A thought that does not get noted is usually lost, so get it down on paper.

Unless your time is cruelly limited, put your material aside for a while, even have another jotting session later. Do not be tempted to solidify anything too early. Quantity is what you should aim at to begin with. Give yourself plenty of options.

Stage two – think, plan

First establish your exact purpose in speaking and get it crystal clear. Is it to inform, to entertain, to persuade? Analyse your purpose – what reaction do you want from your audience? Write your purpose down, rewrite it. Know exactly why you are talking. A talk rarely succeeds if the aim, the objective, the reason for it is woolly and undefined. So get your purpose firmly fixed. Keep it simple and uncomplicated. If you can't write your purpose in a dozen, cogent words, distil it until you can. And have that purpose boldly in front of you from now on, and I mean literally displayed before your eyes all through your preparation.

Now that you have ample material and a glowing purpose, seriously consider for whom and with whom you are going to achieve that purpose. People. Their success is yours, remember. For instance, if it is a technical talk what is their technical level? If it is social talk, such as a club dinner or a wedding, your sole purpose is to make them feel good, to show them that they are special people. Make them feel warm, delightful people, and that what they do has significance and charm. Don't flatter them – but you cannot overdo genuine appreciation of what is good and true about them. The technique of social speaking consists almost entirely of finding a hard core of sentiment and surrounding it with candy floss. So study your audience, the source of the reaction you seek. If you do not know enough about them, find out at once. It is too late to do so when you are on your feet speaking.

The people in your audience are giving you their time and attention. Give them a fair exchange. Your audience is only interested in your subject when it concerns them, so make it concern them. Link everything you say to them and their needs. You cannot do this properly if you haven't done your homework.

Now that you have considered the purpose of your talk and the people you wish to involve in what you say, *find a theme*, a central idea, a banner heading, a motif, a thread to which they (and you) can cling. Keep this theme running throughout your talk. Next, isolate the two or three main points of your talk. Get them completely firm in your mind. Then build the talk around your *purpose*, the *people*, the *theme* and the *main points*. Know what you are going to say and why.

Ninety per cent of a good speech exists before the speaker stands up. Spontaneity needs planning. When the first two preparation stages have been completed – (a) Huge quantities of jottings for raw material, and (b) the audience research and the development of the broad plot for your talk – you should now prepare in detail to deliver your talk to the best effect.

Stage three – you in action

How to begin. Once you are on your feet, don't be in a hurry to launch your opening words. Give your hearers a second or two to stop shuffling and to concentrate on you. Look agreeable. They will respond by being agreeable. Your opening remark must be neither a cliché nor an apology. It must have impact. Make the very first sentence you utter vivid and interesting. They may be expecting the usual bromides. Surprise them a little. Avoid the word 'I' for at least a minute. Substitute 'You' or labels which identify the audience, such as 'Engineers', 'Retailers', 'Architects', 'Housewives', etc; focus on them right from the start.

If your talk is a lecture, do define the limits within which you will be discussing your subject. Give them some signposts. Let them know where you intend to take them and, above all, get them involved. Clearly show, early on, that their interests are in the forefront of your mind and that your subject really has something to do with them. Illustrate your points with local examples from their own environment and experience. Get them involved – at once.

Nerves? What are they? By now you are so busy concentrating on your audience you have forgotten yourself. Now get on with giving them some value.

You know exactly where you are going. Your theme, the few big points. Establish your theme, make your first major point. If your thoughts have been clarified beforehand, the words have clothed them. Just let the ideas flow and let the words look after themselves.

Take a positive interest in your listeners. Carefully watch their early reactions. Are they mentally taking part in what you are saying? Good. Build! Involve them more and more. Nail your first big point on the table. Do not let them miss it. You might feel from time to time that you need to remind them of your theme and the important points. Do so, tactfully.

People have five senses. Don't be an ear basher. Let some of your thoughts reach your audience through their eyes. I recommend that you support at least one of your main points visually. In certain types of talks you can even get them touching (say, material) or even smelling and tasting things. If the circumstances are suitable, use all their senses. Vary your technique of exposition. This sort of activity – picking up things, showing things, moving around purposefully – will also help you personally if you worry about what to do with your hands and body when speaking.

Sometimes it will be good to start your talk with a visual aid, thus occupying your hands until you are able to shift your focus from yourself to other people. One or two simple visual aids can help your audience; seeing is a change from just hearing. It has been said that 82 per cent of all the information we retain comes to us through the eyes. But remember: visual – they must be able to see the point clearly; aid – it must help them to grasp the point. Also, three-dimensional solid objects are preferable to blackboard chalk and talk stuff.

Now, how are you doing? You have opened well, your audience is at ease and confident. They know that your subject concerns them. The lively, interesting manner with which you have presented your first few thoughts has stimulated them to want more. You have planned to give them more. Stick to your theme, stick to your main points. Keep your original purpose firmly in mind and work to achieve it – through them. *Never leave them out of anything you do or say.*

Vary the pace of your voice, vary the pitch. Pauses can have a great effect. Use silence. Don't be afraid to stop to allow the idea to sink in. If you can command attention during a silence, use silence – but sparingly and under control.

Too many notes are a sign of ill-completed preparation

If your theme and your main points are so complicated that you, the expert, need a sheaf of notes to keep you on track, how the devil do you expect your audience to follow you? Clarify. Simplify. Notes belong to the study. They form a barrier between you and your listeners. Learn to do without them while you are speaking. At the very least, reduce them to a bare minimum, say ten key words boldly written in heavy letters about one and a half inches high so that you can see them rapidly – if you really need them.

To sum up:

- Don't worry about speaking – work at it.
- Give your audience a success. Begin with an interesting thought.
- Share everything: your main facts, your theme, your enthusiasm, with your audience. It's their talk.
- Include them in your climactic ending. Finish on a high note: then stop talking. Leave them wanting more.

Here is a checklist for you to work with during your preparation and to keep in mind throughout your talk.

Structure:	Has it a workmanlike shape? Try drawing a graph showing the highlights.
Impact at opening:	Is it alive? Does it intrigue? Does it involve the audience? Does it start an agreeable relationship?
Signposts:	Clear? Brief? Do they indicate where you are all going together? Footholds, map of the route.
Main points:	Facts supporting your proposition: are they justified, authoritative, significant?

Interim summings-up:	Checkpoints. Are your listeners with you, so far?
	Do you need internal signposts?
Final summing-up:	The build-up to the climax. Make main facts unforgettable. Not too long. Involve audience.
Impact at ending:	Restate and achieve your objective. Curtain line stimulating action on their part.
Delivery:	Will they understand your language?
The story line:	Does your narrative include them? Local examples.
	Pictures in their minds?
Audience contact:	Can they see your mind through your eyes? Are you watching, interested in them and their reactions?
Visual aids:	Appropriate? Clear? Simple? Memorable?
Use of voice:	Be generous. Get variety of pitch, pace, volume.
Mannerism:	You've eliminated distractions?
Time:	Are you sufficiently within the time set to allow for more time needed when 'working' the audience?
Them:	Will *they* have a success?

10 Case presentations

Many businessmen and women have to recommend changes that will cost money. In most companies there is a procedure for the approval of capital expenditure. The proposer must begin by preparing a document setting out the proposal in detail. This goes through 'normal channels' and may sometimes be agreed or rejected as it stands. The written part of a proposal is a persuasive report. Approval can be immediate. But frequently the proposer will be asked to appear before some board or committee to present the proposal orally and to answer questions about it.

A case presentation to a board of directors is a combination of:

1 A speech.
2 An interview.
3 A trial at which the jury not only has a vested interest in the verdict but is also the judge on the bench.

Since it is their money you want, you must accept the third aspect as reasonable. There is no appeal. You must win your case first time.

Procedures vary widely but the basic principles apply at all levels. You might need to make adjustments to suit your particular circumstances.

In most worldwide organizations, the uppermost board considers only proposals involving millions or billions. Such cases will have been examined by a lower board and brought upwards by senior representatives of board number two, who in their turn, have heard the proposal from even lower down.

Big fleas have on their backs
Little fleas to bite 'em.
Little fleas have lesser fleas
And so – ad infinitum.

In general, the higher up the scale the smaller quantity of paperwork will be tolerated. Few top men and women care to read more than three pages. They expect their advisers to have taken care of the details and to concentrate on the key issues. These considerations extend to a national or local board who, within the limits of the autonomy granted to them, make decisions without reference to the main board. Let us assume that you are presenting your case to such a board who – may I remind you? – are the jury, the judges and the appeal court. In addition, they are being asked to meet not only the costs but also any damages incurred should your proposal be a dud.

The boardroom is not a playground. Pious hopes and good intentions will get you nowhere. The board's main concern will be: 'What's in it for us?'

When he was Great Britain's Foreign Secretary, the late, lamented Ernest Bevin had occasion to complain that 'he was being sent naked into the conference chamber'. You will, of course, be properly dressed and fully equipped before facing the board. Your career may well depend on how you present your proposal – and yourself.

You will have made yourself aware of the degree of formality required for the occasion. Be courteous but do not overstep the line between respect and sycophancy. A crawler sends out signals that he lacks confidence both in himself and his proposal. You are offering them value for money. Keep that in mind; but there is no need to be either cocky about it or servile. In the knowledge that you have done your homework thoroughly you can be yourself – at your best.

The speech

You will recall that, to be effective, a speaker must stimulate the desired reaction. Nowhere is it more important to understand the minds of an audience than in the boardroom. What's in it for them? must constitute the main driving force of your presentation. What's in it for them? What's in it for them? That is not unreasonable. You cannot expect hardnosed businessmen to unpadlock their wallets merely to replace tears in your begging bowl with company cash. But, you may demur, many companies are well known for their charity.

You will quote, for instance, a grocery chain which provides support for the Arts; or firms who sponsor sporting events; or those who pay for scholarships for students – even retailers who never quibble when you wish to return or to exchange goods bought in their stores. These people are famous for their generosity: it's part of their image. Ponder on that last sentence. Let us applaud their good deeds but bear in mind that givers also deserve rewards and a profit must be seen. That's business. When you make a presentation you will get nothing for nothing. What's in it for them must be your theme. Never be casual in your approach to the decision makers. You want to win: to know precisely what you want before you enter the arena and to leave it having achieved your objective.

Be ready for the fray

Obviously the first question you must consider is: Do I know exactly what I want them to do? Crystallize your objective so clearly that you can define it with a dozen explicit words: shape it so that to motivate action on their part dominates your thinking. Promises are not enough. You want action: but you won't get it on demand. You want something changed. They will want to know your reasons: what is wrong with the present situation – from their point of view?

What is the proposition?

Your opening remarks should be a businesslike statement of the proposition. Do not phrase it in terms of I want (reaction: Oh! Do you?) Find a better way to stimulate their interest. If you can include profit to them in the first sentence, do so, e.g. Ladies and Gentlemen, the proposal is that we should install a new robot system in the coating department at a cost of £485,000 which will produce an extra profit of £128,000 each year after the first two years.

They now know why you have come to them and the sort of money they must have in their minds. Their ears are a-flap at the prospect of this proposal being a good thing for them.

(OK, Mister. We're interested. We heard what you said. Now justify it.)

Note: It might be necessary to use some of your meeting-man techniques as preliminaries to your main statement. Has the chairman set out suitable conditions in his introductory remarks? If he has, be grateful, don't hang about, get on with it. If he has not, you might need to put them into his mind by asking for his guidance. Observe the golden rule. Ask, do not tell him. e.g.:

'Mr Chairman, I propose to explain this matter in about eight minutes. Will that be all right?'

'Yes' he says.

'And you'd rather I answered questions at the end than to interrupt the flow?'

If he says 'Yes' well and good, but if he prefers questions en route, agree with his decision and share another 'Yes' with him.

'With your permission I'll first show what is wrong with the present situation: then how we can put things right and, finally, to draw up a balance sheet to show where the profit comes from.'

'OK' he says. 'That's fine.'

You say: 'Thank you.'

What have you gained?

1   The Chairman's authority to use eight minutes of their time – preferably uninterrupted.
2   The Chairman's agreement to your signposted modus operandi: thus pre-empting, say, the financial director who butts in with a question about money while you are still dealing with production matters.
3   The feeling of the meeting that you are prepared and clearly know what you are about.

Now we get down to business.

Why? Establish a need for change

Here you set out reasons for change from the old to the new. Avoid detail at this stage. Show, by exposing the one, two or three main drawbacks they suffer currently, that they have a need.

This is no time for opinions or assertions. The board will consider only facts – demonstrable facts. They might be aware of some of them and nod their agreement – the yes, yes stream, early development. Try to present your facts in such a manner that they can agree, as you build – fact upon fact, that their present position is untenable. There is a need for change, e.g.:

1   The machines we now operate are twenty-three years old. Maintenance costs are soaring, almost daily stoppages, down-time and idle operators. (*Facts, figures, money.*)
2   Poor finishing, customers' complaints, replacements, rejects and scrapping of inferior parts. Operators and salesmen discontented with their jobs. Within the past year four highly-trained salesmen have resigned and joined a competitor taking with them their/our customer connexions. (*Facts, figures, money.*)
3   The Inspector of Factories has affirmed that we are not conforming to the law regarding safety at work. He says unless we take some action soon, he must. The factory could be closed down. (*Documents, facts, figures, money*)

You have now planted in their minds that their present situation is bad, perhaps even worse than they had thought. Your three main factors demonstrate, in ascending order of compulsion, not only that change is desirable: it is a stark necessity. To take no action could be disastrous. You have opened their minds with the first of three major keys to persuasion – *need*. The second key is their *greed*. The third key is their self-esteem, their status as go-ahead businessmen, caring employers, etc. Need, greed and self-esteem act as powerful persuaders in any presentation. At some time you might have to bring all three to bear: but need is usually enough.

They have now looked at *what* the proposal is and *why* they should change the status quo. Now you ask them to consider the *how*.

How your scheme will work

1 The robot system produces five parts against the three produced by the present machines. The products are of higher quality (samples available). Also, the robots have automatic quality-control mechanisms. Fewer complaints. Customer satisfaction. More sales. Fewer staff problems.
2 Fuel costs are lower. Manpower savings: labour reduced by 40 per cent. Maintenance costs eliminated. The manufacturers will carry out inspection and maintenance for the first five years and offer a warranty to offset (unlikely) stoppages. Down-time negligible.
3 Various options. You and the production manager have investigated four different robot manufacturers, tested their claims and conducted exhaustive trials, personally. The board has full reports on each supplier. For reasons that you have shown in the reports, you recommend supplier Number Two. (One-page summary, tabled.)

Where will the machines be placed

Where is not a problem. There is enough space to install the machines without interfering with current production. Also a much-improved layout will be an added gain.

Who – people

Tread warily. You are on dangerous ground. Many a case has failed because the presenter disregarded the importance of people, especially people like the members of the board. The Personnel Director probably jibbed when you mentioned a reduction in the workforce. Dismissals? Redundancies? How is he going to deal with that? Apart from the unpleasantness, what's it going to cost to lay off 40 per cent of the operators? You've lumbered him with a problem. The Personnel Director's view will become an objection to your proposal. Normally the best time to deal with an objection is to deal with it before it surfaces. If your counter to the objection is sufficiently powerful the objector will remain silent. During your preparation you will need to give much thought to many people. It looks as though several skilled workers might lose their jobs. Do you dwell on this during your main presentation and risk overrunning your time by talking too much? Or do you leave it until question time?

This chapter is based on a real-life incident. The engineer making the presentation had never appeared before the board. He was a member of an in-house speaking course and asked for my help. He worked hard to improve his techniques (see previous chapter) and was not only surprised but delighted to discover that he could address a group with authority and growing confidence. We worked together on his coming board presentation.

- *The what* was straightforward.
- *The why* had the power of solid but dismal facts exposing a daunting need.
- *The how* to solve the board's problem met with their approval.

The engineer and I spent considerable time trying to find an answer to the expected questions about people losing their jobs. The problem seemed insoluble. He mentioned that some operators would be leaving anyway through 'natural wastage'. But that wasn't good enough. Later that evening during an off-duty chat about bowls, he complained that the board was contemplating continuous production necessitating extra shift working and that, he grumbled, would scupper his participation in evening tournaments. 'Hard luck, mate, but glory Hallelujah!' The problem had vanished. Not fewer but more jobs would be created by introducing extra shifts with the new machines. This was now a plus point, not a negative.

Never leave people out of your reckoning. It's surprising what they will do for you if you think about them kindly.

Now the board knows *what* you propose; *why* they need to change the present situation; *how* your scheme will work, and the *who* have been considered. Next you tackle what might be the most difficult part of your presentation:

Money matters

The boardroom is a temple of Mammon, hallowed ground where the moneywise worship. You are in their territory. Respect their rites and customs. Never be casual about money. Directors usually know more about money than do visitors to their shrine. This is no place for bluff, flippancy, guesswork or promises unsupported by facts. The directors will want to see a balance sheet showing:

Expenditure	**Income**
How much of their money you want, and how it will be spent?	How soon they will get their money back, plus a profit – and how much profit?

Do not hurry as they go through the figures with you. Present the broad figures, but have to hand full details should they ask for them. The expenditure part should be straightforward. The income side of the balance will excite more interest. Nobody can be certain of the future. Reasoned probability must be your strength. Your forecasts and estimates must be backed up with concrete facts, e.g.: known performance figures of the machinery, sales and market research etc. Dreams and hopes are out of place. We need something more substantial – forecasts of profits, based on facts – reasoned probability.

When the money has been dealt with and all their questions have been answered satisfactorily, summarize. Briefly remind them of the main points. Oh, do be brief.

Your case is nearly complete. The *what*, the *why*, the *how*, the *who*, the evidence that profits will ensue may have gained their agreement: but you want more than agreement, you want action. Now you must close the deal. Ask for the order, as it were, and get it.

One of the most powerful arguments in favour of action now is that time is not on their side.

When

If you can show that delay will have an adverse effect on their prospects, do so, strongly; perhaps on these lines:

- This very morning, two more customer complaints were received. Goodwill and sales being lost. Money is dropping out of their pockets every day. Action on their part will stop the rot.
- The price of the machines is shortly to be increased by 12 per cent.
- The Inspector of Factories has given final notice that we must, by law, improve safety matters within thirty days. The new system will enable us to avoid serious trouble if we act now.

The close

A good salesman never allows his customer to feel cornered, to feel that they are being sold something. Customers prefer to believe that, on the basis of facts, they have made an intelligent decision to buy.

Do not deliver an ultimatum. Give your board a choice. Assume that they have agreed to the proposal. Now switch ground towards what Churchill called 'Action this day'. The alternatives you put to them are (perhaps):

1 To give you authority to go ahead and order the machines.
2 To arrange for the board to see the machines in action – this week.

Which of these alternatives would they prefer? It is almost certain that they will settle for one of them.

Throughout your presentation you must resist any temptation to show off all you know. Present only what they need to know. If you explore every sidetrack, every nook and cranny, they will not follow you. Stay with them on the main road. Of course they might ask questions about some details. In your preparation you have made ready to answer them with documentary or other evidence.

Sometimes it will help your presentation if you have

consulted a director beforehand to gain his advice on, say, finance or sales. Lobbying – trying to get him to support your proposal in advance – can be dangerous. Ask for facts, no more. If your case is sound, he'll support you, anyway.

Your preparation should also extend to checking on stage management in the board room. Do you know where all the switches are for any equipment you will be using? Are all the document in place, etc? A few minutes with the secretary should be enough to gain assurance on such points. Leave nothing to chance.

Exercise

As a Managing Director, write a set of guidelines for your board, colleagues and staff on: How to prepare for a presentation that will be made to them; and what to look for during such a presentation – strictly from the 'buyers' point of view.

11   Meetings to negotiate

In this chapter you will recognize a combination; a development of your skills as a chairman, as a member, as a presenter, as an organizer. Negotiations test to the full one's ability to handle people at meetings. An expert negotiator is worth his weight in gold.

Negotiations are meetings of minds to obtain agreement and action to satisfy the needs of two or more sides. Agreement is not the same as surrender. Agreement means that both sides see a benefit and act accordingly. Agreement works. Surrender will fester and break out again into worse trouble.

You will never gain agreement during a war: even as a result of a row. The process of agreement can only start when discussion and dialogue replace entrenched 'I'm right and you're wrong' attitudes. In true dialogue, each side must expect not only to change the opponent's mind but to have their own minds changed as well. Many a motorist reaches Heaven ahead of his time as a result of having the right of way and insisting on it too vigorously. Dostoevski in *The Brothers Karamazov* said: 'If people around you are callous and will not hear you, fall down before them and beg their forgiveness, for in truth you are to blame for their not wanting to hear you.'

So your first task is to create the atmosphere in which both sides want to listen as well as talk.

Ninety per cent of the work involved in negotiations must be done before you reach the conference table. Examine the following questions but do so *twice* – first as if you were leading the opposition, A; then B, for your own case. Look at them side by side and do not play down A. Respect their view from the start. At least have that much in common with them.

Please do not merely read these questions. Think them through and answer them honestly – as both A and B.

1 Do you know exactly what you want?
2 Do you really believe in your case?
3 Have you got all the facts that support your case and have you checked them. Facts, not assertions or opinions. *Facts.*
4 What are the strongest arguments for your case?
5 What are the benefits for both sides? (Ideally, the answers to 4 and 5 should be identical.)
6 Why must the present situation be changed – if at all?
7 Who else will be affected?
8 What are the strongest arguments against your plan?
9 What alternative is there; what other options?
10 Have you studied in depth the men and women on the other side?
11 Do you know who your possible allies and strongest opponents are within the other group?
12 Have you done any lobbying? Do you need to?
13 Have you discussed, e.g., the finances or production matters with the experts?
14 Have you prepared handouts of any complicated figures or plans?
15 Are you sure that you have thoroughly mastered the legal side of the matter? Do you fully understand all the organizational rules and regulations which might be pertinent, especially theirs?
16 What is your maximum expectation? What is the acceptable minimum? Where must you stand firm? Are there points of yield or compromise?
17 What timescale is vital? Can you afford to wait?
18 What will be the effect of complete breakdown?
19 Are you ready with contingency plans?
20 What will be the result of total victory for your side – and total defeat for the other – and vice versa? (see Pyrrhic victory).
21 Can you not only settle the current difficulty, amicably but also positively improve the relationship for the future?

A reminder. You should be fully armed with a clear knowledge of both sides before you attempt to negotiate. Major mistakes early on can sink you in deep water for the duration. Don't build a Maginot Line. Recognize that the other side will be ready for you and make certain that you are, at the very least, equally well prepared.

Having gathered all the information available and analysed it thoroughly; having picked out the important facts and factors that will influence the outcome; having closely studied the human relationships involved and the needs of the other side, their strengths, their prejudices, their willingness or otherwise to cooperate, you must now draw up a plan of action both strategic and tactical.

The preliminaries must be organized to create a climate of agreement. Sometimes even a social lunch beforehand is feasible, but of course you must avoid at all costs any suggestion of condescension or bribery. Your aim is to make it clear that you and they are people with a job to do, not antagonists. Nobody wins a war.

You are seeking agreement and, from the start of the conference, it must be clear that this is the purpose of the meeting. The atmosphere must be brisk, businesslike and cordial. The yes, yes, yes technique helps to set the tone. Shape a few early questions or observations to get a 'Yes' response – for instance to get agreement on the purpose, the procedure, the timing and pace, how long have we got for the meeting – an hour, a day, or what? Personal introductions might be necessary. Make them as genial as the circumstances will allow. Get the yes, yes, yes stream started.

Now both parties can proceed on the basis of an agreed objective, an agreed framework for the control and shape of the meeting, an agreed timeframe – yes, yes, yes – so far. Let's keep it that way as far as we can – to the end if possible.

We are not a debating society, we are not in a court of law but we can adapt some of the procedures, some of the disciplines from both to give our negotiations order and shape.

Each side must be allowed to make an opening statement of its views on the matter – uninterrupted. You will of course set a good example by listening, positively. At the appropriate juncture you will ask questions – only for clarification and only to assure them that you have understood their view at this stage. They will, we hope, give you the same courtesy and attention when you present you view. Do not make assumptions or tell them what you think their view is. They'll resent that.

The next step is to establish points of agreement. If possible, avoid going over this ground again, except in summary. Treat what is agreed as a foundation upon which you can build. What will often emerge is that there are only one or two divisive aspects of the matter. Concentrate on these, be as constructive as you can and give them the opportunity to do likewise. Narrow the gaps, build bridges. Show them the benefits through the medium of the facts – even if it is only that they have less to lose, your way. But above all let them talk. Listen. Sometimes they will realize, amid a flood of talk, that they are being irrational in the face of the facts and perhaps suggest a compromise without your asking for it. Note the suggested compromise but don't put too tight a knot on the rope yet; certainly keep your own points of yield in reserve for a while. Reiterate the facts – the one, two or three most powerful facts – and make sure that they are firmly rammed home. The surest way to gain agreement is through self-interest – the other fellows' self interest. Reiterate what they will gain – or lose. There are three keys to influencing people: their need, their greed and their status (self-esteem). Work on all three if necessary. Stay calm. Do not join in a shouting match. Recriminations help nobody.

The Society of Friends set a wonderful example in dealing with stubborn people at meetings. The clerk says: 'Let us have five minutes silence and ask the Lord for his guidance.' At the end of this silence, people are not half so cocksure about their being the only ones in the right. We cannot all use such a method, but a break in the proceedings for a glass or a cup of something often has a calming effect. Better to break off than to have an exchange of insults which are difficult to retract and, of course, divide the parties even more.

Watch your tongue during the break. A stray remark, especially to outsiders – such as the media, can be disastrous.

On the resumption, sum up, emphasizing points so far agreed and spotlight the differences which have to be further discussed. Unpleasantries can be ignored. Get Loudmouth out of the general focus and bring in a more representative speaker to restart negotiations. Both sides should now collectively create a deal which will be reasonably satisfying all round.

You might have to give a bit to get a bit. If you can all come out winning something and agreeing on the course of action to follow you've negotiated successfully.

It is imperative that you record what was agreed and the actions which are to follow. Both sides must formally acknowledge that the record is a fair and joint statement.

Even if you have cause to, resist the temptation to gloat.

Exercise

Please go back to the exercise you did at the end of Chapter 7. Rework it and see by how much you can now improve on your earlier effort. It might surprise you.

12   One-to-one meetings

An encounter across a desk can often make or break a manager. Failure follows almost inevitably if you present your ideas at the wrong time or if you insist on pushing a proposal from your own point of view. Only exceptional men remember technique when it comes to a one-to-one discussion. By all means be relaxed, but before you go in to win your point, or before the other fellow calls on you, do your homework. Get your purpose clear, have your facts ready. Know his problems in relation to your suggestion and start the discussion of the basis of his problems. Until you have established his problems and have shown that you understand them and are in sympathy with them, you must not try to sell him anything. You want him to react, to say 'Yes'. He will not react in your favour if you spend your time putting yourself across. Try it the other way round. Put him and his problems in the forefront. If what you have to sell solves his problems, he'll agree.

Most one-to-one meetings are selling situations: selling goods, selling services, selling ideas – particularly those leading to self-advancement, such as securing a new job or an increase in pay. To stalk into your boss's office on a gloomy Monday morning demanding a rise is not the way to go about it. You will be sensitive to the fact that buyers prefer to believe that they choose to buy rather than they have been sold something.

You already know how to exploit the basics – the other fellow's need, his greed and his self-esteem. An added advantage in one-to-one meetings is that the timing is often in your hands: to await or to create the opportunity, but, above all, to be fully prepared to seize the opportunity when the right moment arrives.

A salesman friend of mine tells the following story with some pride.

During the summer holidays, his son, Daniel, hung about the house, as morose as any twelve-year-old can be with nothing to do but kick his heels. Daniel knew that in about an hour and a half several of father's cronies would arrive for a game of poker and a few beers. Father made it obvious that he would prefer his son to be elsewhere. Father asked: 'Why don't you go over and see Ronnie and the boys?'

The question produced no answer but a pained frown. After a long silence, Daniel sat on the arm of his father's chair.

'Dad,' he said 'nobody could say that you were mean, could they?'

'No, I don't think so' replied father. 'Why do you ask?'

Another silence ensued, until father said, quietly: 'What's the trouble, son? Have you quarrelled with Ronnie, or something?'

'No. Me and Ronnie's all right, but he won't be at home.'

'Well, what about Simon or Tom or one of the others?'

'They'll all be out. Ronnie and them are all going fishing on Maxton lake.'

'Well, you like fishing. Why not go with them?'

'Can't. They've all got bikes, except me. Ronnie says he's surprised that you haven't bought me one like his Dad did.'

'I see. That's what you meant about my being mean, I suppose.'

'No. I don't think you're mean, Dad. You'd buy me a bike if you could afford it.'

'Well, that's no problem.'

'Oh!'

'So you want a bike?'

'It'd be marvellous, Dad. (He produces a catalogue from his pocket.) This is the sort Ronnie's got. They've got one exactly like it at Simpsons in the High Street. Could we go and have a look at it? You've got an hour before your friends arrive.'

Father and son went to Simpsons. They bought the bike. Father glowed with the satisfaction of being a generous sort of chap – at least equal to Ronnie's father.

Daniel went fishing and father enjoyed his poker even more than usual. Both parties gained something.

You will recognize the main selling point: the other fellow's self-esteem. And the close: once father was persuaded to handle the catalogue and to examine the bicycle, action was almost inevitable. It emerged later that the boy had carried the catalogue in his pocket for ten days, waiting and ready for the right moment. His timing was perfect.

There is a time and a place for everything. Add timing to your weaponry.

Father always ends his story by adding, rather smugly: 'My Daniel is a chip off the old block. A born salesman.'

Disciplinary interviews

Disciplinary interviews always have a more beneficial effect if both parties can feel that the discussion was worthwhile and that they gained something. A manager who brays that 'he gave his subordinate a damned good bollocking and sent him away with a flea in his ear' has probably exacerbated the trouble. What you want is that the other man should go back to his work determined not to repeat whatever his offence was. You will not succeed by making him feel less of a man than he was when he came into your office. Nobody suggests that you be a soft touch. To be described by the troops as: 'He's a bastard: but he's a just bastard' is a reputation sought by many an army officer. Justice must be seen to be done. That is more important than a victory for you and defeat for the other.

There are occasions when it is advisable for you to invite a union representative to be present. This prevents a garbled version of the interview reaching the shopfloor. Also you might need a witness should you decide to issue an official verbal warning. This precaution is unnecessary for the less serious offences, but it should be considered at all disciplinary interviews.

As for any meeting: what is your objective? Normally it will be to obtain and to discuss the facts of the matter but, primarily, to ensure that the offence will not recur. You will be courteous and expect courtesy from him. If you are seated, do offer him a chair. Nobody likes to stand wringing his cap in his hands. Supposing that the man's timekeeping is the trouble; you have his time sheet in front of you, but do not wade into him as a prosecutor grilling a hostile witness. Give him a full opportunity to explain his behaviour. Listen. Get the facts. For example he might be having domestic problems necessitating his taking the children to school, thus missing his usual train. Listen. You might be able to help in some way. Let him be made quite clear about the company's point of view. Then deal with the matter is the light of the facts. You know your objective. Achieve it in full if you can: but you might have to give a bit to get much more. Above all, send him away knowing that he has had a fair hearing but deserves all he gets if he is just playing the fool.

The business breakfast

To many people, breakfast is a private sorrow that should be suffered alone – and in silence. The very phrase 'business breakfast' sends a shockwave through their systems. They feel like the worm caught by the early bird. And, often, that feeling truly reflects the situation. Business breakfasts are foisted upon innocents by fellows who revel in too tight a schedule and cram too much into a working day. They rarely form part of the original programme, leaving the victims unprepared and vulnerable.

A Hollywood mogul telephoned a well-known actor inviting him 'to discuss one or two things at breakfast tomorrow morning at Claridges.' The actor, full of hope, travelled up from Brighton. Actors rarely sparkle before noon. This one listened, bleary-eyed, while the mogul waxed autobiographical for what seemed an eternity. Then the mogul's lady friend joined them and business vanished far into the distance. Hiram K, it seemed, had to finish packing. They had a plane to catch. Alone with the lady, the actor was wheedled into promising a free, signed copy of a book he had written and, for the lady's mother, a pair of complimentary tickets for his current, smash-hit play.

And that was the sole outcome of the meeting. Hiram K and his lady departed at the double. The actor never heard from them again.

His agent was furious with him. Of course, he should have been consulted. He knows how to deal with business breakfasts, business luncheons, business dinners and all such chummy ploys as 'Come over to my house, old man. Let's have a drink and a chat.'

Actors are friendly people but they have a gaping chink in their armour. They hate to be 'resting' – out of work, out of sight, unwanted. Even a split week in Barnsley might seem more attractive than waiting at home by the telephone. Employers in the entertainment industry are well aware of this vulnerability and frequently exploit it.

(Enter the agent bearing a shield and thoughts of his percentage.)

The agent is a cynic, hardened by experience. He avows that there is no such thing as a free meal. He will first find out whether there is, perhaps, an ulterior motive behind the invitation. Is there some current reason why his client might be in demand? What's in the wind? If, on investigation, the invitation seems to be purely social, the agent will tell his client to go ahead and be sociable. 'Nevertheless', he adds, 'if you detect the slightest scent of business, don't commit yourself. Refer them to me.'

In truth, of course, we are all vulnerable. We all prefer our talents to be put to work, not resting. As a manager, a stockbroker, a chemist or a clerk; as an engineer or an eager high flyer, you will probably need to be your own agent. You must deal with the apparently casual meeting unaided. Let us by all means be friendly, but let us be prepared to talk business if that's what the meeting is about. Add to your confidence and power by going through all the usual pre-meeting drills. What's the purpose, what's the agenda, what is your personal objective, what are the facts that might affect the issue, what are the options, etc?

The business breakfast, whether we like it or not, is a fact of life. Be prepared. Even if it turns out to be nothing more than bacon and eggs, the exercise of refreshing your meetings drills will sharpen your appetite.

Balls, picnics and parties

All meetings where food and drink and business mix demand a wary approach. Your chances could be sunk without trace by that second bottle of claret or your third liqueur. Four gins before the soup lay foundations for disaster. The grain is incompatible with the grape. In combination, they hate all mankind and pulverize the toughest brain. When the wine is in the wit is out. Forgive me if I sound like a Rechabite but honesty compels me to confess that I learned this lesson the hard way. I pass it on to you to strengthen your power at meetings where laughter is in order – but not from underneath the table.

I had been asked to speak at a formal dinner. Like a drunken motorist who genuinely believes that he is driving rather well, I spoke with alcoholic confidence but finished in a heap. My host, one of the most powerful figures in the business world, being also my boss, sent for me in the morning. I feared the worst, but he was benign and gently smiling. He told me that he had high hopes of me, that I was one of his young lions; then, to my amazement, he asked me to speak at a function a few days hence. He added: 'You will accompany me and learn how to handle a formal social gathering. Remember, you represent both yourself and the company.'

The first thing I learnt, shortly after our arrival, was that my boss was a teetotaller. But he was always to be seen with a glass in his hand, as he moved among the guests. The glass contained an amber liquid that looked like a quadruple Scotch. He fixed me up with a duplicate. 'Don't drink it', he advised 'just sip it occasionally but refuse a refill – except from that particular waiter. He knows what I use and you will use the same. Stay with me and observe.' Dinner was half an hour away.

Have you ever stood aside and cold-bloodedly watched people downing drink after drink, and then some more? It's most educational.

By the time we sat down at the table, several guests were already awash. I felt like a vestal virgin at a bacchanal. Ten minutes before I was due to speak, the boss handed me a large glass of wine, saying, 'That's all you'll get until you've finished your speech. Enjoy yourself.' I did, trying to recall whether it was nectar or ambrosia that was drink for the Gods. This glass of wine was both.

In all modesty, I must record that the speech was a winner and the reception rapturous.

From that evening, I have never taken alcohol before the soup and, if I am to speak, only one glass of wine before I rise.

May I pass my mentor's wisdom on to you? It hurts, but it works.

13 People at meetings

Please consider any giant, multinational company that comes into your mind. Think about its great possessions; the real-estate, the factories, the machinery; the raw materials, the computer system, the stock-in-trade and so on. Also think in terms of money; millions, perhaps billions of dollars, pounds, Deutschmarks, yen – some money going out and more money coming back. That's business. Now take away the people. What have you got? You've got buildings, paper, and lumps of metal. Is that business? Not on your life. The difference between a successful company and a failure is its people – the most important asset of any business.

It is commonplace to regard the management structure of an organization as forming a pyramid. For convenience we will use only one of the pyramid's faces, a triangle: but bear in mind that there are other faces, not visible to the people who work within the confines of their particular slab in their particular triangle.

There is only one position from which all the collective faces can be seen: at the apex. Top people can, and must, look at every aspect of the organization from this dizzy height and

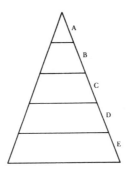

Figure 7

they need to be fully aware of what goes on at each level down to the ground and even to the foundations below ground level. We are told that there is always room at the top. Maybe there is, but space on the pinnacle is viciously limited. There are few comfortable perches up there. Every foothold is a greasy pole. In this competitive world, the unwary receive many a nudge from sharp elbows, even knives, to speed their fall. Success always breeds envy and the venom that goes with it.

What sort of men and women are they, these top people? Envious nitwits rationalize their own failure by equating the acquisition of wealth to sin. 'He's made a fortune so he must be a crook.' 'She's a successful actress, therefore well-acquainted with the casting couch.' This attitude is 98 per cent nonsense (allowing a mere 2 per cent for exceptions to the rule, where calumny is in order.) Success is almost always a reward for hard work, practice, patience, opportunism and the development of inborn talent. Success needs no apology. Nitwit should have his snout thrust into the Bible at Matthew 25, especially verses 14–50, where the highest authority supports the view that talents are not for burying: talents are for procreation, nurture and enrichment.

However, some people are at the top for no other reason than that they were born there. One of the most mischievous of claims is that all men are born equal. If challenged, the claimants add 'in the sight of God' as though they were privy to the mind of the Almighty. The truth is that some people are born to privilege, vast estates and enough money to paper the walls of their mansions with, should they so wish. They are born to power. More importantly, they have, as a birthright, choice and support for what they wish to do with their lives. Those who have talent and also enjoy conditions conducive to its fulfilment are the fortunate few. At the other end of the social scale, a child born in the gutter to poverty and ignorance – even if he had any talent – would find it crushed in the daily struggle to fill his belly. Millions of such frustrated souls have as much chance of success as a barbecued icicle. All men are born equal, my foot!

Despite adversity, some brave ones reach for the stars and make their mark in the echelons of the great. You can, I am sure, think of several examples. Perhaps you are one of them; perhaps on your way. If so, good luck to you.

A perfect egalitarian world would be unbearably dull. Perfection is a full stop leaving no room for variety or adventure. Dreadful thought! Fortunately, most of us have been placed somewhere in between the high and the mighty and the no-hopers: and we are sufficiently flawed to be interesting. We have to make the best of what we've got.

Please take another look at the management triangle. Where do you fit in – at A, B, C or D? Where were you from the beginning and where are you now? Does your progress satisfy you: or does it embarrass you that your boss's boss had to struggle to the surface from far below your base and has passed you en route? The chances are that you have done reasonably well, but, as our school reports used to say: 'he could do better'. We all could. 'But' you ask 'are we not discussing meetings? What have meetings got to do with personal advancement?' The ability to deal with people is the most decisive factor in any career. If you can't handle meetings you can't handle a company.

And here is another hard fact: if you are not actively interested in other people and what motivates them you have no chance whatever to lead and to influence them. Evil men seem to appreciate this fact more than the good. From the small-time confidence trickster to the despot, they make it their business to understand men's minds and how to manipulate them. Gullibility provides their most powerful weapon. They can stir the mob to wave banners and to shout slogans – stir them to the extent that they murder one another in the name of liberty, freedom, religion or other such abstractions. Men rarely go to war for bread, as any villain knows.

'The only condition necessary for the triumph of evil is that good men do nothing.' Let us do what we can in our own cabbage-patch to redress the balance. Your daily round of meetings is not too simple a starting point.

Talent – latent (anagram)

It is an amusing whim that talent and latent are anagrammatical: but these two words evoke a far deeper relationship. Psychologists tell us that we recognize only 10 per cent of our potential power; and of that 10 per cent we actually develop, again, only about 10 per cent. Which means that we use a mere one in a hundred of our given talents. The rest remain latent. You have an enormously greater power than you now employ – power, for instance, to influence people at your business meetings.

So what can one do to develop methods of influencing people at meetings? Let us start at one-to-one meetings, remind ourselves of the basic principles, then extend them to cover the larger meetings – i.e. practise tactics at the smaller meetings and develop strategies for the big ones.

Most people at work take part in dozens of meetings every day without realizing it. If you are not alone, you are at a meeting. Even the most casual of meetings provide you with an opportunity to maintain good relationships, to improve on the less than good ones, to learn something, to share what you know. If you are there, it is your meeting. You are in a position of influence. Let us use the case of Willoughby as an example.

Every department has its Willoughby. It must be admitted that Willoughby lacks charm. It is not enough for Willoughby that he is always in the right: his attitude also suggests that everybody else is in the wrong. Willoughby is incapable of saying 'Good Morning' without making it sound like an accusation. He is the sour apple in the departmental pie. But he is an essential part of the team. His manager, Mr Potter, needs his expertise. Mr Potter dislikes Willoughby, seeks to be rid of him and to replace him with somebody more congenial. With this in mind Mr Potter decides to call on his own director. He makes several mistakes which you will no doubt recognize.

His timing is wrong. Without warning, he drops in on the boss who is busy: but he makes time for Potter. Potter plunges straight in with a request that Willoughby be replaced. The director asks for the facts, meaning the facts as they affect the business: what's wrong with the present situation, the need for change, what advantages does Potter offer to balance the upheaval of replacing a key man – what's in it for the director and the firm? No facts appear; only gripes and opinions. The director asks Potter questions about Willoughby's back-ground. It becomes obvious from Potter's inability to provide details that he has no interest in Willoughby as a member of his staff or as a human being.

The director says: 'I want to think about this. Come in and see me tomorrow morning at ten o'clock. In the meantime, say nothing to Willoughby about this matter. Ten o'clock. OK?'

'Yes, sir' says Potter, and departs.

Question. If you were Potter, what would you do between now and ten o'clock tomorrow morning? What would you do if you were the Director?

The following morning Potter arrives full of hope and with a smile decorating his face. He obviously expects his boss to agree with his suggestion, having thought about it overnight. He is taken aback when the director asks him to represent his proposal now that he, Potter, has had time to think about it overnight. Potter may have had the time, but he has not used it. He flounders. Nothing new emerges. He descends into self-justification by accusing Willoughby of being an introvert and interested in nobody but himself. 'I've even invited him to join me for lunch but he's turned me down. He just gets into his car and disappears. God knows where he eats.'

The director encourages Potter to continue to wade, into deeper water.

'Willoughby's been with the firm longer than I have. The trouble might be that he's jealous about my being brought in and made manager over his head.'

Chin-deep, Potter stops. He looks foolish. He feels foolish. He has, indeed, been foolish.

The director asks, 'Is Willoughby's work satisfactory? Do you find anything wrong with that?'

'No, no, sir. He's very good at his job.'

'Have you got anybody else in mind that could do the job better?'

'Well, no. I hadn't thought it through that far.'

'So it's purely a matter of your personal relationship?'

'Yes, I suppose it is.'

'Have you discussed Willoughby's circumstances with the personnel people?'

'No, sir.'

'I presume that you have, from time to time, studied his personal file to see if it offers any clues.'

'No, sir. I've never seen it.'

'Well you can look at it now. I've got his curriculum vitae

here. Bring your chair alongside mine. We'll examine his cv together.'

'Willoughby is two years older than you – oh yes, I've studied your cv too – he was at a good school, academically he did well. Head boy, captain of both cricket and rugby, school representative on the parent-teacher committee, many other activities. Went up to university – according to one of his references for this job, he was very popular and in line for a blue. Not much sign of an introverted loner –eh, Potter? Did not complete his degree course. Do you know why, Potter?'

'No, sir. Does it say?'

'It doesn't. But I can tell you. His parents were involved in a railway accident. Father died. Mother left permanently disabled. That's where Willoughby goes at lunch time, Potter. Home to tend his mother. He's not anti-social but he has more important things to do. By the way, far from resenting your appointment over his head he turned your job down when I offered it to him. The job entails travel and he had to stay home, anchored.'

Potter moaned: 'Oh, the poor sod. I didn't know. Why didn't he tell me?'

'Some people like to exhibit their wounds. The Willoughbys of this world do not. As we say in the North "There's nowt so queer as folk".'

'Well, surely we can do something about this – get him some help.'

The director beamed. 'That's better, Potter,' he said. 'We might make a manager out of you, after all. The Personnel Director has a few ideas that he wants to discuss with you – about Willoughby, of course.' (He picks up the telephone.) 'George', he says 'I've had a word with Mr Potter. Can you see him now? Good. He's on his way.' (He hangs up.) 'Off you go, Potter.'

'Thank you, sir. I didn't know. . . .'

'It's up to a manager to find out. If you are not actively interested in other people and what motivates them, you have no chance whatsoever to lead and to influence them. Have a good meeting.'

14 The end of the beginning

Dear Harry and Diana; Peter and Anne; Roger and John, et al.

You are far too sensible to believe that you now know it all; that meetings have no more problems for you; that this book, waved over you like a magic wand, has created you Masters of Meetings and Mistresses of the Conference Chamber; that there is nothing left for you to do. The wish, even the resolve to be a better meeting man is a splendid start, but it is not enough. Action on your part is required.

May I make a suggestion that will strengthen your resolve? Earlier, I advised you never to be a mere spectator but always to take an active part and to influence every meeting you attend. On the other hand, is there value to you in the assertion that the onlooker sees most of the game? There certainly is. One can learn much by observing other people at work. I recommend that you make a list of twenty meetings where you can sit in and do nothing but learn by casting a cold eye on the chairmanship, the speakers, the members and the organization of each meeting.

Within a mile or so of any city centre there are probably a hundred meetings going on every day to which the public is admitted. The Courts of Law make a good starting place – magistrates courts, county courts, high courts – all free – are open to you. As a manager or as an employer you should certainly seize the opportunity to obtain vicarious experience of Industrial Tribunals. You might be hauled up in front of one on some future occasion. Public enquiries are always interesting. Local and county councils often prove more lively than one would expect. So, too, do union meetings, church meetings, club meetings, parent-teacher meetings, chambers of commerce and many, many more. There are hundreds of meetings open for your inspection every day.

Make your own selection. Take your checklists with you

and a notebook. Sit back, listen and learn. Then adopt, adapt and improve on every useful idea that you can use within your own sphere of influence. Even inside your own company there are meetings where you are not directly concerned with all the items on the agenda. Take up an observation post at every opportunity. Above all, use and practise what you learn. Increase your know-how and your authority. Grow.

I wish you the best of luck and a lifetime of fruitful meetings.

Yours cordially

Gordon Bell

Gordon Bell

Appendix 1

A short history of Fishbourne & Hawkes, plc, manufacturers of automobile components and accessories. This is a sad tale of clogs to clogs in three generations.

Arthur Fishbourne left school, at the age of fourteen, poverty-stricken and pig-ignorant but with a flair for things mechanical. He could mend a broken clock or get a neighbour's lawnmower going again. So it was natural for Charlie Hawkes to seek his help when the heap of scrap he called a motorbike refused to function. Charlie was considered posh. Sixteen years old, he was still at grammar school and he lived in a house with not only a bathroom but books as well. He also talked posh. More importantly, he offered Arthur five bob to get his machine to work.

Arthur tackled the job with joy in his heart and five bob in his mind – a fortune. He could hardly read and needed Charlie's help to fathom the mysteries of an old motorbike manual. Charlie's father helped, too, by persuading Mr Wills, the owner of the local garage, to let the boys use his workshop. Wills scornfully examined the wreck of a bike and bet Mr Hawkes a pound that it would never again travel ten yards on any road. Arthur asked innumerable questions about what the book said and what the diagrams meant. He wrestled with the bits and pieces, took them apart many times and put them together again: cursed them, coaxed them, fondled them and talked to them like a mother with a sick infant. Then, after sweating four days and nights, he invited Charlie to 'have a go'. Charlie kicked the starter and rode off round the houses. He came back beaming. 'It's lovely' he yelled. 'It works!'

Mr Wills fished a pound note out of his pocket and handed it to Charlie's father.

'Thank you' said Mr Hawkes.

'Not at all' replied Mr Wills. 'I think you might have put me on to something here. What do you know about that boy?'

'Arthur? Oh, he's a good kid; been a pal of Charlie's for years; one of a family of four; father's dead, mother salt of the earth. Pity his schooling has been so awful.'

'Is he still in school?'

'No, he left as soon as it was legal. They need money. He's got to go to work.'

'So you'd recommend him?'

'Without the slightest hesitation.'

'That boy's got the makings of a first-class engineer.'

'You mean you've got a job for him?'

'You bet I have. Can you arrange for me to have a word with his mother?'

Thus it was that Arthur began his career in the burgeoning motorcar industry. Mr Wills, childless, treated him like a son. After ten slogging years of spare-time study and practical work Arthur became a fully-qualified engineer. If a man has talent, integrity, an insatiable appetite for work – and luck – the combination is unbeatable. Mr Wills's business flourished. When the First World War started – sadly, a part of Arthur's luck – Mr Wills obtained sub-contracts which led to major contracts, which led to a massive increase in revenue, larger premises, government support and contact with new ideas and people of great influence. The powers that be decreed Arthur too valuable, making the tools of warfare, to be thrown into the obscenity of the actual fighting. He was 'reserved' and became rich.

No such luck for Charlie Hawkes: he went to the front. When he returned in 1917 he had nothing to show for it but three pips on his shoulders, a small gratuity and one leg missing. But what shows on the surface is not always most important. A good-natured, easy-going youngster went to war. The man that emerged, shaped and toughened by its horrors had developed outstanding qualities of leadership that otherwise might have lain dormant. He also knew from firsthand experience what the army needed in the thick of things. In 1917 men were scarce. Mr Wills offered Charlie a job. Jobs for maimed heroes were also scarce. Charlie joined the firm.

Between 'the war to end all wars' and the next war, the firm prospered. Arthur handled everything to do with production and research. He was rarely seen outside the workshops, blissfully at ease with machinery and machinery men. Charlie became a master of sales and marketing.

Arthur's son, William (Repton and Balliol) took care of finance and personnel. Arthur had married his secretary, a wonderful lady except that she loathed the idea that her son should ever have oily hands – a notion that Arthur reluctantly accepted but never understood. It was a good marriage and they were happy until the day that Arthur, Mr Wills and four senior engineers went to a customer's plant to take part in a test flight of an experimental aircraft. It crashed, killing all on board.

Without its top team of highly-skilled, dedicated engineers, Fishbourne and Hawkes became a bleeding body with a severed head. But they survived. Non-combatants supplying arms during a war need to be stupid indeed if they fail to make a fortune. The crunch came when hostilities ceased.

In 1939 William had bundled off his wife and son, James, to America. She quickly found herself another man and had no intention of returning to a poor, shattered and hungry England. William obtained custody of James. James could hardly be described as a pleasant youth. Having alternately been left to his own devices – neglected – and pampered and spoilt, he also suffered from the effects of a school where the child was king and allowed what was called 'free expression', James proved to be a handful. After years of assiduous private coaching he scraped into a university place. When he was sent down, in his second year, his father had no alternative but to take him into the firm, if only to keep an eye on him. Nepotism gone mad. So much for the past.

You will recall that just now James and his personal assistant Fiona have arranged a management meeting. Please return to the preliminaries of that meeting (page 10).

Appendix 2   Checklists

1   The organizer
2   The chairman
3   Presentations
4   The members

These lists are by no means comprehensive. They frequently overlap. Please add details that relate to your particular circumstances. Retain your checklists and amend them from time to time. If you delegate some duties, see to it that your representative uses a list that meets with your approval. Do not worry about your memory: give it no chance to lapse.

The organizer

- Have you discussed and clarified your brief with whoever authorized or called the meeting?
- Do you know the objective(s) of the meeting? Who will be concerned – how many, what levels of seniority and technical knowledge?
- Is the group homogenous or will it include people from outside the organization, e.g. clients, specialists, union representatives, government officials?
- Will both men and women be present?
- Does anyone need special consideration, e.g. disabled visitors, individual diets, translation facilities, etc?
- Have you investigated and made notes for the chairman and members about people not likely to be known by them?
- Have you booked the conference room well in advance?
- Have you checked it for size, shape, lighting, ventilation,

noise level or other distractions; checked the catering and other services from the location management and staff – given them clear instructions?

- Is all the equipment for presentations on site – and working? Have you discussed details with the operator? Are spare parts available; plenty of material such as transparencies, markers, etc?

Paperwork

- Have all the members received the documentation in good time – agenda, minutes, reports and other papers they need to study beforehand. Are spare copies, handouts, writing materials, folders, available at the meeting?
- Name cards, if required?
- Have you given the participants clear details and as much help as possible about the location and the hotel arrangements that you have, if necessary, made for them?
- Have you arranged for them to be met at, say, the airport and brought to the location – at very least, arranged for them to be greeted on arrival, welcomed and made comfortable?
- Do you have to consider visits or social functions linked with the meeting?
- Have you arranged for the minutes to be taken?
- Have you prepared the chairman's brief after full discussion with him?

The chairman

Ask yourself:

- What is the purpose of the meeting?
- What is the subject (topic) of the meeting and am I sufficiently informed about it?
- Are my terms of reference clear?
- What are the issues to be resolved?
- What actions should result from the meeting: alternative, other options?

- Does the agenda cover the subject and the purpose?
- Which items are likely to be controversial?
- Have I planned a time allowance for each item and got the important matters in early?
- Have all (and only) the right people been invited to the meeting?
- Do I know enough about the members and their needs?
- Will my opening remarks direct the meeting along the right track, establish firm controls and a businesslike atmosphere?
- Have I briefed my staff properly? Have they discussed their duties and reported 'all well' when their part has been done?
- Do I need a chairman's brief?

Reminders

At the meeting, the Chairman must:

- Define the purpose of the meeting,
- Define the limits of the discussion.
- Be impartial, but give some pros and cons to get people thinking and moving towards agreement.
- Keep people to the point.
- Encourage full participation from all members.
- Feed information back to the meeting as required.
- Avoid arguing with members (throw back controversial points to the meeting).
- Sum up where necessary during the meeting.
- Sum up at the end of the meeting; stimulate action.
- Ensure that proper minutes are being recorded.

The presentations

Spoken presentations of reports

In preparing such a presentation, some of the questions the reporter should consider are:

1   What is the purpose of the report?

2   Who are you presenting the report to and what are their special interests?
3   What is their level of technical knowledge?
4   What are the most important points for the listeners?
5   Which items will need detailed explanations?
6   Do your listeners have to make decisions on the report?
7   Have you included all the evidence they need?
8   Which points require visual aids?
9   What questions are your listeners likely to ask?

Case presentation

In preparing a case presentation, some of the questions the proposer should consider are:

1   Do you know exactly what you want?
2   Do you really believe in your case?
3   What are the benefits?
4   Why must the present situation be changed?
5   Who are you presenting your case to?
6   Who else will be affected?
7   What are the strongest arguments for your case?
8   What are the arguments against it?
9   What alternatives are there?
10 Have you got all the facts that support your case, and checked them?
11 Have you done any lobbying?
12 Where necessary, have you discussed the financial details with the specialists?
13 Do you know who your probable allies or opponents are?
14 Have you prepared hand-outs of any complicated figures?
15 Have you considered how you can get action immediately?

Members of the meeting

Before the meeting, the members must consider:

•   The points on the agenda.

- The action the meeting is intended to produce.
- Supporting documents required.
- The likely attitudes and alignments of the Chairman and the other members.
- Whether to lobby any other members for their support.

The members must ask themselves:

- Am I clear about what my contribution should be?
- What information do I need from others?
- What information are others likely to need from me?
- Have I the authority to agree to decisions reached?
- Do I know who is likely to support me, and who is not?
- What points must I stick to?
- Where can I compromise?
- What action do I want from the meeting?

At the meeting, the members must:

- Keep to the agenda and limits set by the Chairman.
- Approach the meeting objectively.
- Work towards constructive solutions to any problems that arise.

If the Chairman and members have prepared on these lines, a meeting should succeed.

Meetings are composed of people, not angels. The Chairman must be tolerant, but firm. He (or she) must occasionally remind members that the good of the company is more important than the good of the individual. He should try to keep people in a constructive frame of mind. He must never humiliate; and in controversial matters he must always leave people a ladder to climb down. The Chairman must keep things moving, and make it plain to members that the meeting is not going to waste time. *The key word in business meetings should be 'business'.*

Appendix 3   Recommended reading

Bell, Gordon (1987), *The Secrets of Successful Speaking and Business Presentations*, Heinemann Professional Publishing.

Citrine, Norman (1982), *ABC of Chairmanship*, MCLC Publishing.

Seekings, David (1989), *Effective Conferences and Meetings*, Kogan Page.

Ward, Sue (1982), *A to Z of Meetings*, Pluto Press.

Yelland, John (1982), *The Conduct of Meetings*, Rose Jordan.

Index